Rhythms of Grace
Experiencing the Rhythmic flow of the Gospel
Scott Bryant

A GRACE REVOLUTION

*There is a sound flowing throughout the church and the world.
That sound is "The Rhythm of Grace." Are you listening?*

Dedication

To my wife, Meg, who gave me the inspiration to write this book; I am an incredibly blessed man to live my life with you. Each day is our adventure with Him.

TABLE OF CONTENTS

Dedication..4

I. UNDERSTANDING THE GOSPEL OF GRACE

CHAPTER ONE-   Finding Our Rhythm 9

CHAPTER TWO-   Between 2 Laughs................................ 19

CHAPTER THREE-   Breaking it Down.................................29

CHAPTER FOUR-   Ebb & Flow..37

II. EMBRACING THE GOSPEL OF GRACE

CHAPTER FIVE-   We've Got Rhythm, How Bout You?....47

CHAPTER SIX-   Finding the Right Balance......................57

CHAPTER SEVEN-   The Tie That Binds................................65

CHAPTER EIGHT-   Embrace the Grace................................73

III. LIVING THE GOSPEL OF GRACE

CHAPTER NINE-   The Cadence of Grace..........................83

CHAPTER TEN-   No More Blurred Lines..........................91

CHAPTER ELEVEN-   Yolo...99

CHAPTER TWELVE-   Bethany, Would You Say Grace?...........109

Unless otherwise noted, all scriptures are from the English Standard Version of the Bible. (ESV)

RHYTHMS OF GRACE

Experiencing the rhythmic flow of the Gospel

Part I

Understanding the Gospel of Grace

1

Finding our Rhythm

Extraordinary afflictions are not always the punishment of extraordinary sins, but sometimes the trial of extraordinary graces. – **Matthew Henry**

There is a subtle cadence that exists in things all around us. It is a current that connects life, through beats and breath, minutes and seconds, conversation and even silence. This flows in everything we know. Rhythm.

Rhythm is everywhere. It is in the cadence of a platoon of marching soldiers, and in the thump-thump of your heart as you experience excitement or fear. It is in the sounds of waves at the beach and of a passing train.

It is in our daily routines, in our relationships, on our jobs, in our schools, and in our churches. It is in our homes, our community, our country, and all throughout our world.

Rhythm.

Then however, there are more subtle rhythms. There are the rhythms of silence between the sounds. It is here, in the tiny spaces where you think nothing exists, that we find the greatest rhythms of all.

It is here that we find the silent tempo that calls us to know and to be known by a Holy and Righteous God.

They are the Rhythms of Grace. They are moments that take our breath away in awe of God's wonder. These rhythms do not have to be extravagant or even things that are seared into our memory bank forever, but they are spaces in life that shape our destiny.

A few months ago my wife posted a scripture on a certain social media site to encourage friends and family. I am sure at the time; she had no idea how far that single act of selflessness would reach, nor did I.

Here is what she posted.

Matthew 11:28-30
"Are you tired? Worn out? Burned out on religion?
Come to me. Get away with me and you'll recover your life.
I'll show you how to take a real rest. Walk with me and work with me—watch how I do it.
Learn the unforced rhythms of grace.
I won't lay anything heavy or ill fitting on you. Keep company with me and you'll learn to live freely and lightly." (ref. Msg)

Sometimes it is hard to see the richness of scripture without knowing the full context. Have you ever begun watching a favorite television show, and the first scene seems like you have missed something?

As you continue to watch though, you find that the story

rolls back to the beginning and flows from there. That form of narrative is called *in media res*. (Latin: "in the midst of things")

It is a narrative technique that has been used from the 9th century B.C. to the present day. The purpose of *in medias res* is to open the story with dramatic action rather than exposition. It sets up the situation, then as the story unfolds, flashes back to illuminate and explain earlier events.

That's how we are going to look at, and come to understand, the **Rhythms of Grace.** My prayer is we will see flashes of the rhythms of grace in our lives. We will see moments that God has revealed Himself and His grace and then we will begin to truly see that He has taken every step of the journey with us; and that His plan involves every detail of our life.

In the following chapters we will dive deeply into this text, but for now I want to focus on just 3 words - Rhythms of Grace.

One definition of the word rhythm according to the Merriam-Webster Dictionary is, *"movement, fluctuation, or variation marked by the regular recurrence or natural flow of related elements."*

Also, one of the definitions for grace in the same dictionary is, *"unmerited divine assistance given humans for their regeneration or sanctification."*

So when we speak of the **Rhythms of Grace** you could say *that they are marked by the regular recurrence or* **natural flow** *of undeserved divine assistance given for our* **regeneration** *and* **sanctification**. (My paraphrase) (ref. Merriam-Webster)

Now that we a definition for the rhythms of grace, let's look at the story leading up to those wonderful words in **Matthew**

11:28-30. The story begins with Jesus and John the Baptist.

Matthew 11

Vss. 1-3 *"After Jesus had finished instructing his twelve disciples, he went on from there to teach and preach in the towns of Galilee.*
² When John, who was in prison, heard about the deeds of the Messiah, he sent his disciples ³ to ask him, "Are you the one who is to come, or should we expect someone else?" (ref. NIV)

So here we are. John the Baptist is in prison for preaching and baptizing. He sends word to Jesus. "Hey, are you the one?" Remember he called Jesus, *"…the lamb of God who takes away the sins of the world."*

What happened to make him question this now?
He is in jail! That is what! He is looking at the four walls of a prison cell. That probably is not how he saw his ministry going. No big salary package, no book tours, no conference bookings. Nope, John goes to jail.
So he sends word to Jesus, "Is it really you?" Because this is not how I saw this thing playing out? Jesus sends word back to him making reference to the prophet Isaiah.

Vss. 4-5 "⁴ *And Jesus answered them, "Go and tell John what you hear and see:* ⁵ *the blind receive their sight and the lame walk, lepers are cleansed and the deaf hear, and the dead are raised up, and the poor have good news preached to them."*

His reference comes from **Isaiah 61**. He says the blind

receive sight (check), the lame walk (check), lepers are cleansed (check), the deaf hear (check), the dead are raised (check), and good news is preached to the poor (check).

But wait.

Jesus left one thing out. He didn't mention that he came to set the captive free. What? Hey Jesus, you left one out. A very important one if you ask John. Then Jesus goes on to say...

Vs.6 *" ⁶ And blessed is the one who is not offended by me."*
OUCH!

Could you imagine being the messenger that had to take this back to John?

Would he repeat what Jesus said verbatim? Or after passing the news, what would he say then? What would he say to comfort John? What would you say? What Paul said?

Romans 8:28 - *"And we know that all things work together for good to them that love God, to them who are the called according to his purpose."*

How do you think John would have reacted? He probably would have punched him in the nose and said, "I guess that was for your good, bro." Things didn't look good for John then, and things weren't going to get any better, not in the natural life anyway.

Now we know John loved God, and we know that he was called according to God's purpose, so what do we do with that? We do what John did. We trust God. We trust the rhythms of Grace.

If you've ever had trouble accepting the sovereignty of God, and His plans, just look at John and all he had on his plate (pun not intended). John was having a bad day, and it had to be hard for him to see God's plan in this. But there are some very important principles to be noted here.

The *"Rhythms of Grace"* flow in two primary streams. These are not exclusive but are primary. They are for…

Regeneration- God is all about regeneration. Both in the heart of man and in all the cosmic creation. First, the plan of salvation starts with the human heart, renewing that which was damaged in the fall of man. Also, is at work in renewing the entire creation of God, which also suffered with the fall. Basically regeneration's purpose is to "reverse the curse", not only on a personal scale, but on a cosmic one as well.

Sanctification- Dr. David Osborn said, *"Too often we try to use God to change our circumstances, while Christ is using our circumstances to change us."* (Compass Magazine, April 2003)

You see, God is right now in the process of making us like Christ.

Think of the process of refining maple syrup. Maple trees are tapped with buckets hung under the taps, and out drips a sap, which is thin and clear, like water. On a good day, 50 trees will yield 30-40 gallons of sap, but it is essentially useless at this point with only a hint of sweetness.

Then as the buckets fill, they are emptied into large bins that sit over an open fire. The sap comes to a slow boil; and as it boils, its water content is reduced and its sugars are concentrated. Hours later, it has developed a rich flavor and golden-brown color, but it must be strained several times to remove impurities before being reheated, bottled, and graded for quality. In the end, those 30-40 gallons of sap are reduced to one gallon of pure, delicious maple syrup, which is far better than the cheap, imitation, colored sugar-water that represents maple syrup in the grocery store.

So it is when we come to faith in Christ. We start like raw, unfinished sap, which could have been tossed aside as worthless. But God knew what he could make of us. He sought and found us, and his skillful hands are transforming us into something precious, sweet and useful. The long and often painful refining process brings forth a pure, genuine disciple easily distinguished from cheap imitations. *(Michele Straubel, Red Lake, Minnesota. From a sermon by C. Philip Green, Our Living Hope, 4/26/2011)*

A great illustration of sanctification on every level is found in:

2 Peter 3:11-13 *"¹¹ Since **all these things** are thus to be dissolved, what sort of people ought you to be in lives of holiness and godliness, ¹² waiting for and hastening the coming of the day of God, because of which the heavens will be set on fire and dissolved, and the heavenly bodies will melt as they burn! ¹³ But according to his promise we are waiting **for new heavens and a new earth in which righteousness dwells.**"*

The word *dissolved* in this text is often misinterpreted as destroyed, when the more accurate description is that of a refining fire. In this refining fire impurities are removed, and the pure, "righteousness is left to dwell."

You see, both regeneration and sanctification are working toward a much more permanent plan than anything we can imagine. They are working toward a place where righteousness dwells, a promised place, anticipated by the groans of all creation. They are working toward eternity.

We might see Jesus' response to John as insensitive or cruel but it was anything but that. The greatest thing we can ever do is **ANYTHING** God wants us to do, and then spend most of our energy and focus on planning for our permanent place of residence in eternity.

It is when we look at the glass as half full, we see that John had a very successful ministry, with countless lives made aware of the Messiah. He caused many to see their sin and need for a Savior, and signaled the arrival of Christ

And the Rhythms of Grace continue.

But we are still working on context and have yet to arrive at the main point. Just when John's disciples thought Jesus was being insensitive, he moved into a dialogue of encouragement and affirmation.

Vss. 7-11 *"As John's disciples were leaving, Jesus began to speak to the crowd about John: "What did you go out into the wilderness to see? A reed swayed by the wind? [8] If not, what did you go out to see? A man dressed in fine clothes? No, those who wear fine clothes are in kings' palaces.[9] Then what did you go out to see? A prophet? Yes, I tell you, and more than a prophet. [10] This is the one about whom it is written:*

'I will send my messenger ahead of you,
who will prepare your way before you.'

[11] **Truly I tell you, among those born of women there has not risen anyone greater than John the Baptist;** *yet whoever is least in the kingdom of heaven is greater than he."*

I knew a man who used to say, "Second hand praise is the most affirming of praise." At first I had a hard time with that thought. I wondered if he was just saying that to avoid giving first hand affirmation. Some people are like that. They are afraid affirmation, or praise of others, makes them appear weak, so they never offer it.

That came to my attention one day while I was talking with a consultant working with the church. He told me about a huge compliment that my pastor gave me. It was not until that moment that I understood the power of second hand praise. If someone thinks enough about you to tell other people, then that person thinks pretty highly of you.

John received that kind of praise from the one who created the heavens, the earth, and everything in it.

WOW!!!

Knowing that Jesus said that about me would turn any bad day around. Right? John was having a bad day, and then there came word that John had been laying up treasures in heaven. He had been making preparations for eternity, not by his works, but by living out his purpose. He was preparing the way of the Lord.

Now that's a high calling, and soon he would be enjoying the splendors of Heaven himself. Not all things were good, but Christ was working all things toward the eternal good.

And the Rhythms of Grace continue.

Rhythms of Grace point us to a greater plan than ours, not our will but the will of God in Christ.

Have you seen the Rhythms of Grace in your life?

Have you prayed for things, only to thank God later that He didn't answer that particular prayer?

Or have you learned the hard way to wait for God's plan to develop in a situation?

I know I have. So be encouraged. Throughout this book, we will look at how the Rhythms of God's Grace work in our lives and how they have worked in the lives of many men and women in the Bible. I encourage you to read prayerfully and let God show you how the fullness of His grace has worked itself out in your life and the lives of those around you.

Between Two Laughs

We are either in the process of resisting God's truth or in the process of being shaped and molded by his truth. **-Charles Stanley**

Several years ago, I was in a church service when a funny thing happened. I didn't just happen into this service; I was not speaking at the service. I was a part of a men's discipleship ministry for men struggling with addictions and other life-controlling issues. I was new to authentic Christianity (and believe me, there is a faux version). I was taking my time and allowing God to change me at His pace.

During the service the minister called me forward. If this has never happened to you, you've missed out on one of the most uncomfortable, awkward moments, a person can experience.

When I got to the front of the room, he began to speak over my life some things that God had shown him about me. He began to tell me that God was going to use me to reach thousands of people with the Gospel and that I would be able to reach people that the average minister never could. I will always remember those words. He encouraged me to write them down but I didn't need to. I completely understood the part about being able to reach those the average minister never could. I have a past riddled with drugs, prison, and other sins that most ministers have not experienced. I'm in no way saying that to brag about my past. My past is just that - My past.

I am saying that I believed that I could approach almost anyone and carry on a conversation without making that person feel uncomfortable, but the other part of what he said just made me laugh!

How would God ever use me to reach thousands with the Gospel? I had very limited knowledge of the Gospel, had never been to seminary, and I had no platform for that kind of impact.

I laughed to myself thinking, well God, either this guy missed it, or you have your work cut out for You. But no matter how unbelievable I thought this declaration was, I couldn't shake the fact that God spoke to me through this young minister.

At the time I was unaware that a similar declaration had been made to someone in scripture, who also found it unbelievable.

And no, it wasn't a tattooed guy with a tainted past, it was an elderly woman named Sarah. You see, Sarai (later called Sarah) and her husband Abram (later called Abraham) were asked to leave their home and go where God directed. God said He would make a great nation from their family. The only problem was, they had no children.

She was 65 years old and Abram was 75.

So when we fast-forward 24 more years and after a failed attempt to make it happen on their own, we find the beautiful couple a little doubtful.

Just when the promise had all but vanished from the mind of

this precious couple, they had a visit from 3 strangers in Genesis chapter 18.

They prepared a meal for the strangers, and while Abraham was entertaining the guests, they told him that in one year his wife Sarah would have their long awaited child. Please understand Abraham was 99 years old, which meant Sarah was 89. So when she overheard the conversation from inside the tent, she laughed.

I completely understand. When we are told something so hard to believe, it's difficult to think that since God said it, that settles it. We have finite, pragmatic minds that can't see the possibility of impossibilities. That's not how God sees things. He specializes in the impossible. And it helps to look at stories like Sarah's and mine from the outside and say, "Just trust God".

Believe me, I get it now.

But when you are the one in the impossible situation, things seem a little different. Can you relate to this?

Have you ever been facing an impossible situation, only to get a word from God that everything is going to work out?

Well, in my situation, I wish I could tell you that I woke up the next morning a preacher of the Gospel who spoke to thousands of people, but that's not exactly how it went down.

A few months later, I got a job at our church- as the janitor; but I wasn't laughing anymore. I began to see God working in my life on His plan. I was able to study more.

I started taking classes at a local Bible College for ordination to become a minister. Then one day our pastor had to go out of town on short notice and he was unable to get a guest speaker to replace him, so you know what? He called me.

That Sunday I preached the Gospel to over 600 people. That was just the first of many more Sundays during which I was able to minister to lots of people.

The first few times that I spoke, I threw my guts up from nerves, but today I look back and laugh at the goodness of God.

A couple of years ago I ran into that same young minister that spoke those words over me. I told him the whole story, and we laughed together.

Now let's go back to the story of Sarah and Abraham. Remember she laughed when the Lord said she would have a child in just one year. Now she is 90 years old and we pick up the story in Genesis chapter 21. Let's just read what the Bible says…

Genesis 21:1-6 *"The LORD visited Sarah as he had said, and the LORD did to Sarah as he had promised. [2] And Sarah conceived and bore Abraham a son in his old age at the time of which God had spoken to him. [3] Abraham called the name of his son who was born to him, whom Sarah bore him, Isaac. [4] And Abraham circumcised his son Isaac when he was eight days old, as God had commanded him. [5] Abraham was a hundred years old when his son Isaac was born to him. [6] And Sarah said,* **"God has made laughter for me; everyone who hears will laugh over me."**

Did you catch that? She said God has made laughter for me and that laughter will make everyone who hears laugh.

So we have times WHEN we laugh, and then times WHERE we LAUGH!!! And we find the Rhythms of Grace "Between the Two Laughs".

Destiny is in the Dash

There are three distinct parts of a promise from God.

First, there is the ***promise***, which sometimes sparks that first laugh, that time when you think to yourself, "Anything short of God doing this, and it's going to flop."

Then, there is the fulfillment of the promise. That's when we see the second laugh. When we see that God cannot fail. He will never fail. That is not not how God rolls.

In *between the two laughs* is the most important component of the promise. **The Dash**. The *dash* is the space *between the two laughs*.

Claude Debussy said, "Music is the space between notes".

And the space between the two laughs is where the music of our lives resonates. Between the laughs is when we have to trust, we have to exercise faith, and we have to be patient.

James 1:3-4 *" knowing that the testing of your faith produces patience. 4 But let patience have its perfect work, that you may be perfect and complete, lacking nothing." (ref.NKJV)*

There is an uncertain period of time between the two laughs that tests our faith and tries our patience. Being human, we usually miss a very important key in this process. We will tend to either...

Focus too much on the promise- this may cause us to become proud, entitled, and lazy. These things can cause us to freeze in the now, while daydreaming how awesome we are going to be when this promise comes to pass.

Joseph fell into this trap (literally) in the book of Genesis. He had a dream and became proud of who he would become. The morning after, he woke up, ran to the kitchen and proudly told his brothers of his dream.

They were so excited for him, that they decided to kill him, and would have succeeded had it not been for his brother Reuben, who talked them into throwing him into a pit instead.

We can cause more problems for ourselves than solutions if pride is a result of the promise. Or we…

Focus too much on getting to the payoff- This is a silly thing but we all do it.

We create scenarios of what life will look like when God fulfills His promise. Our main problem is not that we want to see it happen, our problem is when we don't see it happen fast enough, we tend to try and work it out ourselves.

We use phrases like, "God helps those who help themselves," right? Well, there is only one problem with that statement.

THE BIBLE!

If we had been able to help ourselves, Jesus wouldn't have had to go to the cross.

Romans 5:8 *" …but God shows his love for us in that while we were still sinners, Christ died for us."*

While we were still undeserving of God's grace, while we were still sinners, Christ, the Son of God died for us, making opportunity for us to be in right standing with a holy and righteous God. We could never fix that, but Christ fixed it for us through the Rhythms of His Grace.

Still we have a tendency to try and fix things.

Remember Sarah? Now whether it was her idea or Abraham's

is up for debate, but either way, they tried to help God out to fulfill His promise. Abraham would sleep with Sarah's maid, and the maid would have the promised child. Well, she DID have a child, but NOT God's promised child.

Not only did they not accomplish what they intended, but can you imagine how awkward it was around the house after that?

We see then, if too much focus on the promise can cause problems for us, and too much focus on the payoff can work against us as well, then there must be a way to do this that will be for our good.

So what do we do?

We embrace the process- Remember, "the music is the space between the notes." God has us right where we are now because He is working out things in us we don't yet comprehend.

He's working things out in your situation, and He's working things out in you.

The weight of true destiny would crush the immature. So God uses tests of our faith to produce patience, and patience to work towards our maturity.

James 1:3-4 says "...*let patience have it's perfect work.*"

The word perfect there is **teleios** in Greek which means- (a) complete in all its parts, (b) full grown, of full age, (c) especially the completeness of Christian character.

Our job is to ***embrace the process***. Embrace your "now."

If you are a pizza delivery guy, then try to be the best pizza delivery guy the world has ever known. Have a great attitude in all you do, no matter what you do.

So many people forfeit or give up on the promise because the process becomes too much for them.

Your spouse still doesn't want to go to church? Don't give up! Your teenager seems to have lost their mind (remember yourself as a teen)? Don't give up!

Your boss overlooks all your accomplishments, and magnifies your failures? Don't give up!

Galatians 6:9- *"And let us not grow weary of doing good, for in due season we will reap, if we do not give up."*

Don't give up. Don't give in. **DO NOT SETTLE** for less than God promised. Ask God to remind you of the promise from time to time. That way we don't ADD to the promise. We don't allow our flesh to re-create the promise, but we allow God to get us ready for it. God is preparing us for what He's already prepared for us. However, you might say, "If it's God's promise, He can skip the process and just give me the end result."

The process is pointless.

The process isn't pointless- ***the process is the point!***

The process is where we learn why our spouse doesn't like going to church and we listen and allow God to use us to bring the Gospel of Grace to him/her. That's when we exercise the love of God towards our teenager and allow God to work out His salvation in their heart. Our living out real Christianity every day is the most effective tool in our tool belt. If someone see's Christ in you, then they will be much more open to hearing about Christ from you. It's a process.

That's where you have a chance to rise above petty circumstances at work. You can love your boss, even if he/she doesn't feel the same way. We can be encouragement to those around us. We can let the light of Christ shine in a dark situation.

God will show his might by working things out in others *through you*. He is working things out in you to strengthen your character! And through it all, we begin to see the importance of the process. It makes us more mature.

It makes us **teleios** - - *(a) complete in all its parts, (b) full grown, of full age, (c) specially of the completeness of Christian character.*

1st Laugh ~ 2nd Laugh

The process is the place where character is developed. It is where we learn to lean into God's Grace for our sanity as well as our sanctification. In the process we learn to trust God and His sovereign plan for our lives. In the process we have the choice to either allow God to use us to help others along the way or to see ourselves as the center of the universe.

Often, we think our problems are huge and we feel others should get on our pity bandwagon, but God is busy making us into the image of His son. So look to Jesus' example of embracing the process no matter how tough it is; God is using it for His purpose, and that purpose is always bigger than just you.

If we embrace the process, and allow God to mold and shape our character, then we can stand strong in the promise God made. So don't faint in the process, the music is the space between the notes. ***Your destiny is in the dash***.

Breaking it Down

The whole is greater than the sum of its parts. - **Aristotle**

I love the way the Message Bible interprets Matthew 11:28-30. It is so descriptive of the original text. It digs down deep into the story Jesus is telling, and the context in which it is being told. It is such a wonderful picture of Grace.

Matthew 11:28-30- *"Are you tired? Worn out? Burned out on religion? Come to me. Get away with me and you'll recover your life. I'll show you how to take a real rest. Walk with me and work with me—watch how I do it. Learn the unforced rhythms of grace. I won't lay anything heavy or ill-fitting on you. Keep company with me and you'll learn to live freely and lightly." (ref. MSG)*

Of all the memories I have, some of the greatest ones come from my childhood, but not because my childhood was without problems.

I grew up like a lot of people.

My family put the "funk in dysfunction," not too much, and

not too little. My life consisted of good days (mostly due to other people) and bad days (mostly of my own doing).

But one thing that makes me nostalgic of the *"good old days"* is that those days were so stress free.

Of course I had the "burden" of wanting to have the coolest pair of parachute pants, penny loafers, or whatever was 'in' that week. I also had to deal with the relational stress of losing the girlfriend(s) I would never be able to live without, but overall my days were light and easy. I loved those days. Then life eventually began to get heavier and heavier.

I tried church.

My grandmother used to drag me to church (spank or not to spank, that was the question.) But church did not do it for me, and the older I got, the more cynical I grew towards church, or more to the point, towards *church people?*

Life was getting pretty heavy.

When Jesus gives us the invitation to come to Him in Matthew 11, He invites those who are tired, those who are worn out, even those who are burnt out on religion to come to Him. There's no laundry list of do's and don'ts. His invitation is simple.

Come.

I wish I would have grasped this truth earlier, but I did not.

As the years went by, the weight of the world began to increase. Older people warned me about my behavior, but what did old people know?

Right?

Well, it turns out that they knew a lot more than I gave them credit for. But I did not listen to them, nor did I listen to the invitation Christ was giving me.

Oh *I heard* it almost every Sunday in church, I just did not listen. The longer I ignored Christ, the heavier the weights got.

When I was approaching my teenage years I began to understand how heavy these weights were becoming. I had lost both of my grandfathers and my uncle in just over two years. That was tough for me, but as heavy as those losses were, I felt they were still manageable.

However, shortly thereafter, my father passed away and my world spun out of control. I didn't show it on the outside; guys just didn't do that. But on the inside, I had a heaviness that I couldn't shake.

Fathers are those people who can answer questions that you can't ask anyone else.

Not even mom. And I have a great mom.

I have an AWESOME mom!

She did her very best to be mom and dad, but even she could not take away the weight. Over the next few years I tried **extreme measures** to relieve myself of that weight.

I tried teenage rebellion. That didn't help. As I grew older, I tried alcohol. It was fun, but it didn't help. It actually added more weight. So I finally tried drugs. Then, I thought I had found the answer. While high on drugs, the weight just floated away. However, when the drugs wore off, the weight was there again, only heavier this time.

It took a long time, some of it spent in prison, and a lot more weight added to the pile I was already carrying, and then one day I heard Christ's invitation.

Not only did I hear it, but also I listened, and not only did I listen, but I responded.

No stipulations, no lists of things I needed to accomplish first, no strings attached whatsoever. *Just come.*

So I went. And guess what? It was true.

It was all true.

All I had to do was come to Christ.

He said, "...*Get away with me and you'll recover your life. I'll show you how to take a real rest...*"

When I came to Christ I felt the weights lifted, I had my life back, and I was able to rest like I hadn't rested since childhood. Only Christ is able to give rest and restoration at the same time.

So if you are tired, worn out, or burnt out on religion, Christ is extending an invitation to you right now. Will you come to Him? If so, the best is yet to come.

Then the text says, "Walk with me and work with me—watch how I do it." This is where it gets interesting. To get the full effect of this, let us look at the same idea in the English Standard Bible translation.

Matthew 11:28-30 "*28 Come to me, all who labor and are heavy laden, and I will give you rest. 29 Take my yoke upon you, and learn from me, for I am gentle and lowly in heart, and you will find rest for your souls. 30 For my yoke is easy, and my burden is light.*"

We've covered verse 28 already, but we must look to see why the message translation covers all the bases.

The first part of verse 29 explains the picture in verse 28.

I will focus on "*29 Take my yoke upon you, and learn from me...*"

At the time Jesus said this, a Jewish audience would have understood the use of the phrase 'take my yoke upon you.' Yoke was a common metaphor for a rabbi's interpretation and application of the Torah. This was the first five books of the Bible- the Written Torah (Torah Shebichtav) and the Oral Torah (Torah Shebe'al Peh).

When a disciple began to follow a rabbi, "they took up their yoke" and committed to living out the yoke or teachings of that rabbi. So Jesus says, "Take my yoke upon you, and learn from me..."

Historically the yoke of the Torah, or the law, had proven impossible to keep. People tried, and people failed. It is a tiring process to try to do something that is impossible to do.

You get tired, worn out, even burnt out on religion.

So you see, the Message version really breaks these verses down for us. When he says, "walk with me," He means that every step you take, he'll be there to walk alongside you. When he says, " work with me," He is saying that there will be work, but that work will flow from a regenerate heart, a relationship with Christ, not the law.

It will be the desire of our heart, not compulsion. And when He says, "watch how I do it," He is not only telling us how, He is going to show us. He will always be our example.

1 Peter 2:21 *"²¹ For to this you have been called, because Christ also suffered for you, leaving you an example, so that you might follow in his steps."*

Jesus doesn't want to burden us with do's and don'ts. He wants us to follow Him, to follow His example. Where the law illuminated sin in our lives, Jesus wants to illuminate our lives.

John 1:4 *"In him was life, and that life was the light of men."*

Now moving back to our text, we come to the crux of this entire book.

This is big- HUGE!!!
"LEARN THE UNFORCED RHYTHMS OF GRACE."

Grace is one of the most powerful words in scripture, but it is also seen by many as one of the most dangerous words relating to Biblical teaching.

As soon as you mention Grace, or more specifically the Gospel of Grace, certain people freak!

Here are some of the things that are said...
- Grace leads to rampant sin.
- People will abuse the Grace of God.
- Grace is good, but too much Grace leads to trouble.

The apostle Paul anticipated the same reaction from the religious community of his own day after he said,

Romans 5:20- *"Where sin abounded, grace abounded much more"* (ref. NKJV).

He asked the question he expected us to ask:

Romans 6:1- *"Shall we continue in sin that grace may abound?"* (ref. NKJV)

Should we sin so that we can receive more grace? In other words, "If people believed what you just said in Romans 5, Paul, wouldn't they take advantage of the situation and live anyway they wanted, knowing they were safe and secure from the wrath of God?"

Good question.

However, it reveals a basic misunderstanding of the nature of God's saving Grace. Paul answered simply: *"Certainly not? How shall we who died to sin live any longer in it?"* (ref. Rm. 6:2)

In this Paul speaks plainly, *have you died to sin or not?*

You might think that would have been sufficient to answer questions about the possible abuse of God's Grace, but it wasn't.

So let's go deeper.

The Greek word for Grace used in the New Testament is the word *charis* from which we get the word *charisma*. Thayer's Lexicon says this word is used 122 times in the New American Standard Bible and 131 times in the King James Version using the meaning of Grace we are discussing here.

That seems like it might be a very important thing. As a matter of fact, **Grace** is used more times in the New Testament than the word ***sin***.

So on which one do you think God wants us to place more of our focus? Grace or sin?

Let's look at how one of our fathers of the faith answered that question.

Someone confronted Martin Luther, upon the Reformer's rediscovery of the biblical doctrine of justification, with the remark, "If this is true, a person could simply live as he pleased!" "Indeed!" answered Luther. "Now, what pleases you?"
(ref. Michael Horton, The Agony of Deceit, Moody Press, 1990, pp. 143-144.)

That says it all. What pleases you?

> If Christ paid for our sins on the cross, which ones did He pay for? Only the ones we confess? What if you forget one? How far do we need to go back and confess?

Or does He forgive all the sins leading up to our conversion, and then it's our responsibility to confess each one from that moment on?

Let me ask you a question. If any of those situations were the case, what would our mind be on?

Grace or sin?

Which one should we think on more often?

Now don't get me wrong, we need to live a repentant life, but we need to realize Grace doesn't make it acceptable to sin, it makes us want to live for the one who **PAID HIS LIFE FOR OUR SIN.**

Grace should make us want to live life to the fullest for the glory of Christ.

We must learn the *Rhythms of Grace*.

We must learn that the same power that raised Christ from the dead is available to us by faith. That power saves us, and that same power is available to us in an unending rhythmic flow.

That power is Grace, and Christ wants us to come to Him just as we are, whether we are tired, worn out, or burnt out on religion. He wants us to come to Him and receive a new life.

Not a life of bondage, but a life of freedom in Him.

He bids us to work with Him, as a result of our walk with Him, and to walk with Him in the same manner He walked according to the will of the Father.

And as we walk, He will continually teach us the wonderful *Rhythms of Grace.*

The Gospel of Grace isn't heavy, or ill fitting. Christ promises freedom from sin, and He delivers.

Our job is to walk in that freedom.

When we keep company with Him, He will teach us how to live life to the fullest, and to live our lives honoring the price He paid for our freedom.

Slowly but surely our lives begin to flow in rhythm.

Let me ask you this, do you have rhythm?

4

We got Rhythm how 'bout you?

Rhythm is something you either have or don't have, but when you have it, you have it all over. - **Elvis Presley**

Let me ask you a question. Can you dance? I bet you said yes. So let me ask you another question. If I were there with you, and there were quite a few people standing around, how would you answer that same question?

It is amazing how many people when asked simply say they can't dance. When the truth of the matter is, almost everyone can dance. Dancing only requires two things:

> **The ability to move**- No matter what your situation is, if you are reading this book, you have the ability to move. Even if your movement is very limited, you can move.
>
> **The ability to hear the beat**- Can you snap your fingers, tap your foot, or clap your hands to the beat of a song?
>
> Well it's starting to look like you have the ability to dance.

So you see, most people are capable of dancing. And dancing feels good.

But even though our dancing feels good to us, it does not

necessarily feel good for everyone. It may be funny, but it is not very pleasing to the eye. Some of us just do not have rhythm.

When I was in school, we used to have these rallies between school bands at the football games. Our team would play a selection while the cheerleaders and students danced, then we would say, "We got rhythm yes we do, we got rhythm, how 'bout you?" And then the other team would give it their best shot. We always thought we had better rhythm.

Well, this same scenario plays itself out when people look for the Rhythms of Grace in the scriptures.

Many think Grace is for the New Testament. They think it is a now thing, that began with the Gospel. The New Testament has Rhythm, but not the Old Testament. That was the time of the law, so Grace wasn't a part of that time. If that is how we understand it, then we need to do some re-thinking.

It is sad that ministers of God's Grace will leave out any teaching from the Old Testament when dealing with the topic of Grace, because this leads to a fragmented view of God's character and of the Gospel of Grace.

As we are going to see, God's grace not only appears in the Old Testament, but it pre-dates even the law in scripture.

2 Timothy 1:9 *"He has saved us and called us to a holy life--not because of anything we have done but because of his own **purpose and grace**. This **grace** was given us in Christ Jesus **before the beginning of time**,"*

This verse says Grace was given in Christ before the beginning of time. That's further back than we can trace, so let's look as far back as we possibly can and see what we find.

Adam

In Genesis 1 God created everything and everything He created He called good. The Hebrew word for good is the word…

" Tob" *delightful,* ***favorable, gracious***

Then on the sixth day God did something amazing. He said "let us make man in our image". Then He formed man from the dust of the earth.

Out of all the creation, God took the time to use His hands to personally shape man into His own image.

He expressed unmerited favor towards man.

We did not deserve God's special attention.

Not only did He shape and form man with His hands, but also He breathed the breath of life into the nostrils of Adam. God's love and His Grace were manifested even in the creation. And when the day was done, God looked back and said, "It is VERY GOOD".

The very act of God Himself breathing the breath of life into man reveals the intimate relationship that He desired to have with us.

When God breathed the breath of life into Adam, He also imparted to him a special spiritual essence, called the "spirit in man" (Job 32:8; 33:4; Zech 12:1; I Cor. 2:9-11), giving him the unique ability to think and reason, and to acquire knowledge to make decisions, based on that knowledge.

At the same time, God also implanted into Adam's mind a fully functioning language in order that he might communicate with his Creator.

Then to show the importance of a close intimate relationship, God made woman for man.

They shared the Grace and fellowship with God in the perfect place He had made for them. Grace was evident in the life of man.

But that perfect situation did not last. The *fall of man* happened and though things progressively got worse, God's grace never left the scene.

Noah

In Genesis 6, things had gotten pretty rough, and people were choosing to do whatever they felt like doing. In the midst of a sinful world with whom God had all but lost patience, He places his gaze upon a man named Noah.

The Bible says Noah found Grace in the eyes of the Lord (Gen. 6:8). When God could have easily destroyed everything and started fresh, He chose Noah's family to keep the Rhythms of His Grace flowing.

Through this one family He would not just rebuild but establish His people. These people would follow Him and make more people, and eventually God would bring forth from them a son, through whom would come the redemption of the world.

God protected this family and provided for them during a catastrophe that wiped out the rest of planet earth. We know the story of Noah and the Ark. So we know that the story of Noah is a wonderful picture of God Grace. In this story God cleanses the earth and the rhythm continues.

Abraham

Next we see God's Grace in the life of Abraham (known as Abram at the time).

Abraham was called by God (an act of Grace,) and was commanded, "Go from your country, and from your kindred, and from your father's house. Go to a land that I will show you, and

I will make of you a great nation, and I will bless you (also an act of Grace from God), and make your name great; and YOU SHALL BE A BLESSING; and I will bless them that bless you, and curse him that curses you: and in you shall ALL FAMILIES OF THE EARTH BE BLESSED (a prophetic picture of Grace to come through Christ).

Through Abraham and his son Isaac (remember Sarah who conceived him when she was 90,) God's blessings were passed on to Jacob, whose descendants grew to become the twelve tribes of Israel.

Today we continue to see the fulfillment of this promise. God's people have a special place on the global landscape. We continue to see God protect and bless His people all around the world. The wonderful news in this revelation is that we, as believers, are heirs of these blessings. You can choose for yourself to be one of God's people. That is the flow of the Rhythm of God's Grace.

Moses

Through grace and mercy, God delivered the children of Israel from their slavery in Egypt.

God called Moses to lead them out of captivity in Egypt and into the Promised Land, and He gave them His commandments so that they might continue to receive His blessings and Grace.

It is very important that we see what God is up to in all of this. God's desire was to dwell in the heart of mankind. To do that, He would need to become a man.

Sin had caused a breach in that relationship, but God is smart. He chose a people, that would be His people, and through those people He would choose a woman to have a child, His child, and that child would be Him.

So God selected Moses to be the deliverer and shepherd of His people through a season of trial in the wilderness.

Moses himself found grace in the eyes of God, when he pleaded with God on behalf of the children of Israel after all their sins and idolatry, which they had committed while Moses was gone up to receive the law on Mount Sinai for forty days and nights.

Exodus 33:12-16 *"And Moses said unto the Lord, 'See, You say unto me, "Bring up this people"....Yet You have said, "I know you by name, and you have also found grace in My sight." Now therefore, I pray You, if I have found grace in Your sight, show me now Your way, that I may know You, that I may find grace in Your sight: and consider that this nation is Your people....For wherein shall it be known here that I and Your people have found grace in Your sight?'"*

During this time God gave the people the law.

Now note: most people have a problem with either the law or with grace, but God makes it really clear. The law served a wonderful purpose. During the time of testing in the wilderness, the law gave people a choice to either be His people or not.

The law was a fence around God's people. Remember He had to protect His "surrogate", because she would give birth to God as a man, and that child would bring redemption to the entire world. The law protected God's seed for an appointed time so you and I could receive His Grace.

As the story continues, Moses led the children of Israel to the Promised Land, and in that land, many years later, God chose a woman to have a baby of God's own people. God's Grace took every step with them.

God continued to show His Grace in the lives of men like,

Joshua, Gideon, Samuel, David, and many more, but Grace was not exclusive to men.

Women like Sarah, Rachael, Rahab, Deborah, Ruth, and many more were shown God's favor throughout their lives and the lives of their families. God protected His people in exile, and when they found their way to the Promised Land, He kept them separate and holy.

One of these stories of God's Grace in exile is found in the book of Esther.

Esther

In this story, the children of Israel were in captivity under Persian rule. One of the Persian leaders hated the Israelites and wanted nothing more than to mistreat or kill them.

However, one young girl named Esther, according to chapter 2 verse 17 of the book of Esther, found Grace in the king's eyes. That Grace later gave her audience with the king that resulted in the salvation and favor of the children of Israel.

God's Grace was also evident in the life of the prophets Daniel, Jonah, Isaiah, and in the lives of Jeremiah & Ezekiel. Through the lives of these prophets, God gave His children pictures of not only the Grace that was available then, but of the Grace to come. Look at this...

1 Peter 1:10-12- "*[10] Concerning this salvation, the prophets who prophesied **about the grace** that was to be yours searched and inquired carefully, [11] inquiring what person or time the Spirit of Christ in them was indicating when he predicted the sufferings of Christ and the subsequent glories. [12] **It was revealed to them** that they were serving not themselves **but you**, in the things that have now been announced to you through those who preached **the good news** to you by the Holy*

Spirit sent from heaven, things into which angels long to look."

Are you beginning to see a pattern?

A pattern of God graciously reaching and pouring out unmerited favor upon a man or woman who would love and obey Him.

Do you notice that all these people had two things in common? They all received the blessings and favor of God (Grace), and as long as they were obeying God, the Rhythms of Grace flowed in their lives.

The entire Old Testament is filled with stories of God's Grace bestowed on those who sought God with all their hearts. To those who ignored or rejected Him, they brought upon themselves punishment and wrath for their sins.

So when we think of the Grace of God, we can't look at the Old Testament and say, "We got rhythm how 'bout you?"

We have to realize that even though the men and women of the Old Testament looked like they couldn't dance, we must remember, everyone can dance.

God wants our love, our obedience; He wants all of our attention.

When we are mindful of His wishes, the Rhythms of Grace flow like rivers in our lives.

We begin to dance.

Rhythms of Grace
Experiencing the rhythmic flow of the Gospel

Part II
Embracing the Gospel of Grace

5

Ebb & Flow

Action and reaction, ebb and flow, trial and error, change - this is the rhythm of living. Out of our over-confidence, fear; out of our fear, clearer vision, fresh hope. And out of hope, progress. - **Bruce Barton**

The one thing certain about rhythm is there is a flow to it. That flow sometimes takes us to the top of the mountain, but at other times we must trek through the valleys of life (metaphorically speaking). This rhythm, as we've previously discussed, has purpose. It will usually strengthen our resolve and develop our character. If we were honest with each other and ourselves, we would prefer to stay on top of the world. We love mountaintop experiences.

Recently, we took a few days vacation and went to the beach. It was an incredible trip. My wife and I were invited to stay at a condo with my mom for a few days. Each day I would take a long walk with my mom, and we would just walk and talk about life. It was refreshing and the time would just fly by. I'm not really sure how far we walked but it was so cool that I knew my wife would have to join us the next day. Sure enough we talked her into it and we all went for a long walk one afternoon.

However, this time I got the bright idea that I would walk down the beach and while they were talking, I would wade out into the surf and swim back alongside them. Now if you know me, this won't shock you at all. I'm notorious for acting before I think. You see, the current of the waves move at an angle, and that angle was moving against me as I swam. I tried to swim out further hoping to get past the waves a little so I could keep up with their stride. It didn't work.

I worked, harder and harder to keep the pace, but the more time went by, the further behind I got. They weren't trying to leave me behind, they were just moving at a normal comfortable pace. I was fighting against the rhythm of the tide, and I was losing the fight.

As I fought those waves, I began to wonder how many people experience the same thing in their everyday lives. We have seasons in our lives that appear to be like leisurely strolls. The time passes as we move from blessing to blessing, from Grace to Grace and we feel as one standing on a mountaintop saying, "Surely I have arrived."

But life doesn't let us stay there does it? So why can't we just stay there? Why can't we just stay on the mountain? Let me try and answer that with another question. Have you ever had a long season of being on the mountain? I have and I'm sure you have too. What happened? I will almost guarantee the result was **ROUTINE.**

There are a lot of dangers to the Christian walk, but routine is one of the most dangerous. A.W. Tozer said one of the most treacherous enemies of the Christian and of the Church is the dictatorship of routine. We know what happens next, because it is a routine.

"The routine dictates, and we can tell not only what will happen next

Sunday, but what will occur next month and, if things do not improve, what will take place next year.

Then we have reached the place where WHAT HAS BEEN determines WHAT IS, and WHAT IS determines WHAT WILL BE."

[A. W. Tozer. "Rut, Rot or Revival: The Problem of Change and Breaking Out of the Status Quo." Compiled by James L. Snyder (Camp Hill, Pennsylvania: Christian Pub. Inc., 1993]

Routine isn't an easy place to move from. It's comfortable. There is no tension in routine, but there is no progression in it either and God is the God of forward motion.

He is the God of progression.

Just look at the Bible, it starts with a garden and ends with a city.

That's progression.

So I found myself fighting those waves and asking why all this tension, when I realized the tension was making me more resilient and actually helping me to grow stronger. I realized in that moment that it was GRACE giving me the strength to keep going and it was GRACE taking every stroke with me.

So where are you now?

Standing atop the mountain?

In the valley?

Or in the process of either moving up or down the mountain?

Go tell it from the Mountain

Everyone likes to be on top of the mountain. When we look at scripture, it is easy to think people are closest to God on top of the mountain. Think about it.

Let's look at a couple of literal examples in the Bible.

When Moses was on the top of Mount Sinai, he saw

God. God spoke with him and gave him the law. But as much as Moses must have desired to stay on the mountain with God, he couldn't. The children of Israel had grown impatient and were drifting into sin. So Moses had to leave the mountaintop to return and bring to the people of Israel what God had given him on the mountain.

(my paraphrase of **Exodus chapters 19-32**)

The Prophet Elijah found himself on a mountaintop for a completely different reason. He was discouraged because none of God's warnings had caused king Ahab or Jezebel to repent for their sins. And to ice the cake, Jezebel sent word to Elijah that she was going to have him killed. His flight from death landed him atop the same mountain that Moses had been on. And guess what? God visited him there. God came to Elijah on the mountain to encourage and refresh him so he could go down and bring to God's people what God had deposited in him on the mountain. (my paraphrase of **1Kings 19**)

Do you see the pattern? We have literal examples to show us how God brings us to spiritual mountaintops, not for us to remain, but so He can deposit something in us that we can share with others. But that deposit isn't law. It is GRACE.

John 1:17- *"For the law was given through Moses, but grace and truth came through Jesus Christ."*

As good as it feels to be on the mountain, we must know we are there for a reason. We must avoid distractions, pride, and complacency. We must know that it is by Grace that we are there, and it is for grace that we are commissioned to go back down. Have you noticed that nothing grows on the top of high mountains? If you travel to the peak of a very high mountain, you will usually only find rocks and snow, but that's about it. Even the snow, as it melts, flows down from the mountaintop.

Down in the Valley

That melted snow forms a mountain stream that moves down the mountain and into the valley.

A valley often starts as a downward fold between two higher places. But as the water flows downhill it begins to erode the rock and create a depression (low place) to allow the water to gather and form a river in the valley. That's the natural flow of things, but it's also the supernatural flow as well. The mountaintop seasons fill us up so that we can be poured out in the valley.

If you speak "Christianese" at all, you have heard reference to mountaintop and valley experiences. Most of the time the valley gets a bad rap. The valley seems to be a place of desolation, a place of loneliness, a place of loss, and even a place of desperation. But the valley has great purpose. Rivers and streams flow in the valley, so things grow in the valley.

I think one of our biggest problems with the valley, and probably the thing that causes us to miss out on the benefits of the valley, is our perspective of it.

We usually look at things like this topographically. We only see it as high and low. If this is our perspective then the valley always looks depressing, because it's a depression (low place).

We are frightened of valleys in our life because we think of them as rock bottom, but there is a way of looking at valleys that will bring a healthy perspective to our vision.

We can choose to not only look at them topographically but also geographically as well. We can look at the lay of the land.

The entrance to the valley is a very wide place between two

hills or mountains. This place is called the "head" also called the "entrance". Then the smallest point in the valley that is usually the end is called the "gorge" but often called the "throat."

Sometimes we enter the valley seasons of our lives in our "head" (or mind) and often things get really cramped or uncomfortable just before we come out the other side through the "throat" with the power of our words.

You see the valley begins with the "head" and ends with the "throat." The only other way out of the valley is UP!!!

I'm not saying that we need to act like the valley isn't there. It is, but if we see God's Grace flow in the valley, then we will grow in the valley.

2 Corinthians 9:8 -*"⁸ And God is able to make all grace abound to you, so that having all sufficiency in all things **at all times**, you may abound in every good work."*

We are...
Saved by grace
Forgiven by grace
Kept by grace
Healed by grace
Freed by grace
Restored by grace
Called by grace
Transformed by grace
We are to live by Grace
So that we may grow in Grace

Don't get lost in Transition

Sometimes we find ourselves on the mountaintops in life, other times we find ourselves in the valleys, but there are those times between the two.

These are points of transition. These points of transition are more ambiguous than others, so in these seasons we really need to lean on the Grace of God for our strength as well as our sanity.

In seasons of transition, we are neither on the mountaintop nor in the valley. We are not where we used to be but we have not yet arrived at where we are destined to go.

When we look around, we tend to get frustrated because the landscape doesn't reflect where we think we should be. But, these seasons play equally important roles in our lives.

A great example of this is the life of the Apostle Peter.

He was present at Caesarea Philippi where Jesus asked, " who do men say the son of man is?"

Everyone was eager to answer, but Peter answered, "you are the Christ…" at which Jesus says Peter will be a rock on which the church will be built. This is a huge mountaintop moment for Peter.

But only verses later Jesus tells Peter, "get behind me Satan". At that point it doesn't matter how great you feel, that statement will knock you from the mountaintop all the way to the valley.

Later during the last supper we find Peter in a state of transition. Jesus tells the disciples that someone at the table eating with them will betray Him. This statement threw all the disciples into a state of transition. And this gives us a picture of how we all react in a time of transition.

At first they began to ask, "Who could it be?" They looked for the obvious- Blame someone else.

Next they began the process of elimination, not by evidence, but by trying to figure out who is the greatest. Each said, "It couldn't be me, I'm so AWESOME."

But Jesus took this moment to explain to them the Rhythms of Grace. He said my Kingdom of Grace works contrary to the world system. The world says the one who is served is the greatest, but Grace says the one who does the serving will hold the seat of honor. The thing you need is the Gospel of Grace, and that is something you simply cannot earn.

Then He turns His attention to Peter. Peter isn't on the mountain now, but he is with Jesus so he isn't exactly in the valley. He's in transition. Jesus says in...

Luke 22:31- *"Simon, Simon, behold, Satan demanded to have you, that he might **sift you like wheat...***

In Peter's mind he had to think, "Well what are you going to do about that Jesus? Surely you won't allow that to happen." So Jesus says in verse 32
"but I have prayed for you that your faith may not fail. And when you have turned again, strengthen your brothers."

This is where we learn about transition. Jesus didn't cast Satan away. He didn't stop the sifting, but He gave Peter assurance of his task after the sifting.

The sifting is the process of the transition.

Look at the process of the sifting of wheat. When wheat is sifted, it is shaken, it is tossed, it takes a beating. But the process of sifting wheat works to remove the things that aren't beneficial to the body. The waste is removed, and the fruitful things remain. The same happens to us.

Many times seasons of transition seem tough. We seem to be

shaken, tossed about, or even abused, but it is so important that our faith doesn't fail. It is our faith that is pleasing to God, and it is through faith that we receive Grace, and that Grace sets our life back in rhythm.

Seasons of transition will remove those things that are not fruitful for the Body of Christ.

Hebrews 12:27 -*"Yet once more," indicates the removal of things that are shaken—that is, things that have been made—in order that* ***the things that cannot be shaken may remain."***

So whether we find ourselves in a mountaintop season, a season in the valley, or in a season of transition, we know that these seasons are serving a purpose for our destiny.

God is moving us along a progressive path.

Contrary to popular belief, life isn't best measured topographically (ups and downs) but is best measured theographically. Let me explain:

Theo- *a combining form meaning "God," used in the formation of compound words.*

Graphic- *of, relating to, or represented by. Described in vivid detail. Clearly outlined or set forth.*

Theographic-Living requires walking by faith and not by sight. When we walk this way, our lives are ***vividly detailed by God*** and the Rhythms of Grace flow.

6

Finding the right Balance

A grace-starved, truth-starved world needs Jesus, full of grace and truth.
–Randy Alcorn

Recently I was asked by a friend to meet with a young man struggling with drug addiction and alcoholism. As unqualified as I am, I've dealt with both those problems and today I've lived more than 8 years addiction free, and I meet regularly with men struggling with many life controlling issues, but that isn't the main reason my friend asked me to meet with him. He is an atheist (actually a secular humanist) and my friend thought we could possibly have some interesting dialogue.

I met with the guy and he's an incredible person. We hit it off and I consider our friendship a progressively good one, but the first day we were hanging out, he was a little inebriated. He asked me how I could possibly believe that the Bible is true. I won't go into the details but it spun towards some very intellectual morality topics questioning the nature and character of God. My answer was simple- GRACE.

"What?" he said. "That doesn't answer my question at all."

My response, "You're asking the wrong question."

That might sound silly to you, it definitely did him, but many of us go through life asking the wrong questions, especially questions concerning Grace.

There is much controversy surrounding the Gospel of Grace in the church today, but if you look at the church historically, you'll find that this isn't abnormal. Anytime God releases a reforming revelation to His church, it is usually met with either aggressive skepticism or attacked as heresy.

Grace itself isn't the problem with most Christians. We understand that Grace saves us, so that very limited view of Grace is easy to grab, but many people frown upon the radical message of Grace. The radical message of Grace says the cross is a FINISHED work, but this message seems too extreme for many. Here are just a few statements you will encounter in the church today when you mention Radical Grace...

- People will go crazy in sin if you preach too much Grace.
- Grace will eventually be abused.
- You can preach Grace, but you need to balance it with Law.
- Grace takes all the responsibility away from the Christian.

The list goes on and on, but these proclamations lean toward a "works" based lifestyle. If you don't know what's wrong with that, then we have some work to do (pun intended!)

First, let's look at some scripture to address the statements above.

Will we really go crazy in sin if we trust in *Radical Grace?*

Romans 6:14 -*"For sin will have no dominion over you, since you are not under law but under grace."*

Well, what about the abuse of Grace?

Romans 6:1 – *"What shall we say then? Are we to continue in sin that grace may abound? ² By no means! How can we who died to sin still live in it?"*

Max Lucado said in a recent interview, "When grace is appropriately received, it actually creates a DESIRE to do good—not permission to do wrong."(ref. Grace the Empowers. A conversation with Max Lucado by Erin Gieschen In Touch)

Shouldn't we balance Law and Grace?

You see. There we go, asking the wrong question. Here's what I mean.

John 1:14-17- *"And the Word became flesh and dwelt among us, and we have seen his glory, glory as of the only Son from the Father,* **full of grace and truth**. *¹⁵ (John bore witness about him, and cried out, "This was he of whom I said, 'He who comes after me ranks before me, because he was before me.'") ¹⁶ For from his fullness we have all received, grace upon grace. ¹⁷ For* **the law was given** *through Moses;* **grace and truth** *came through Jesus Christ."*

Grace and Law aren't even two different sides of the same coin as many people think. They are two different coins all together.

In scripture, specific times are separated by Dispensations.

Dispensation- "a general state or ordering of things; specifically: a system of revealed commands and promises regulating human affairs."

The Law was given to God's people through Moses ending the Dispensation of Promise (not the promise, but the dispensation) and beginning the Dispensation of the Law.

God had established His people, and now He was giving His people a chance to simply obey Him and walk in the fullness of His Promise.

So the dispensation of Law was given and the dispensation of Promise was fulfilled.

God promised Abram that He would make of him a great nation. And then God began to create that nation. The Law was given and the people of God were distinguished from other nations by their keeping of the Law. So the Law served the purpose of keeping the Israelites from sin. It made them set apart from the rest of the people on earth (the Gentiles), fulfilling the Promise made to Abraham.

The Dispensation of Law then continued for hundreds of years. Then Jesus came and began to talk about a new Dispensation. But that Dispensation wasn't to condemn the Law. Look what He says in…

Matthew 5:17 – *"Do not think that I have come to abolish the Law or the Prophets; I have not come to abolish them but to fulfill them. "*

What Dispensation would fulfill the Law?

When Jesus went to the cross, the Dispensation of Law was fulfilled and the Dispensation of Grace began.

So when we read "…the Law was given through Moses, Grace and Truth came through Jesus Christ", we see that it is Grace and Truth, not Grace and Law that Jesus came to present to mankind.

We have the Law in one hand, and Grace and Truth in the other. The latter (Grace and Truth), came to fulfill the former (The Law) in Christ Jesus.

It is very important to know that Jesus didn't just bring Grace, but He brought Grace and Truth. This is key because Jesus is full of Grace and Truth: Either one without the other and you don't have Jesus.

That is a major problem in the church today. Even Grace preachers miss this one. It's all about Grace, so we preach Grace and the finished work of the cross. That's perfectly true. The work of the cross is a finished work. Jesus didn't mince words in...

John 19:30 – *"When Jesus had received the sour wine, he said, **"It is finished,"** and he bowed his head and gave up his spirit."*

This allows us to break free of the works mentality of the law, which says, "DO".

We then receive the gift of God's Grace that says, "DONE". I will never forget the first message I heard on Radical Grace. Wow!

I felt as if this amazing wind of revelation had blown upon the church, and the wind continues to blow. I couldn't get enough of Grace. I began to dig into the scriptures with a new fire.

Grace was everywhere and I began to digest everything I could read or listen to, and discuss with others.

What I found were some that felt as I did.

God was releasing this new season upon the church and if we could just grab it, the routine (or religion) would fall away and we could grasp the Gospel like never before.

Others, I found, were repelled by the Radical message of Grace saying things like those we saw earlier in this chapter.

But I felt as if I'd jumped into the boat of Grace and began to sail into the sea of Gospel freedom.

My problem, however, was if God was giving this incredible revelation to the church, why was there so much division among the ranks?

My conclusion was too many people were either...

- **Confusing Truth and Law-** They knew there was more to it than just simply casting out to the sea of freedom with no checks or balances. Their fears were that history would continue to repeat itself with people abusing the wonderful blessings of God. But Jesus didn't bring the law, He brought Grace and Truth.

Or they...

- **Embrace the Grace and forget the Truth.**

John 14:16-17- "And I will ask the Father, and he will give you another Helper, to be with you forever, 17 even the Spirit of Truth, whom the world cannot receive, because it neither sees him nor knows him. You know him, for he dwells with you and will be in you."

I received this wonderful Gospel of Grace and jumped into the boat floating into this beautiful freedom.

Yet this is only half the equation.

Grace is freeing and we cannot change the power of Grace no matter what we think. Grace pushes the boat forward into a wonderfully free future, but we read that Grace and Truth came in Jesus Christ.

So how does Truth fit in the boat of Grace?

Truth controls the steering. A boat without a rudder just floats in the water aimlessly. Jesus brought Grace, which says that the work of the Gospel is a finished work.

If we jump into the boat without Truth, we begin to realize that the boat has no steering.

We can trust in the Grace and know that all things will work together for the good. We will eventually arrive at our destination if we don't crash into the rocks; but God didn't design our lives to be lost on the sea of freedom.

God placed destiny in us and destiny has the same prefix as the word destination.

The Gospel of Grace is moving us toward destiny and the Spirit of Truth is our guide (or rudder).

John 16:13- *"When the **Spirit of Truth** comes, he will guide you into all the truth, for he will not speak on his own authority, but whatever he hears he will speak, and he will declare to **you the things that are to come.**"*

My wife and I have a little dog named Abby. She is a *Bichon Frise* (not very masculine but she's ours.) She is growing old and has diabetes so her eyesight is getting worse. When I walk her it's always an adventure. She has always had a lot of energy, so when we walk she walks very fast, sniffing the ground.

Her life is a perfect picture of Grace. She loves freedom and she is so excited to just explore. But there is one small problem; she can't see where she's going. I am so thankful for the invention of the leash. Now I am sure some pet owners would disagree, but those owners have obviously never had a pet with poor eyesight.

If I were to let Abby outside to run free, she would enjoy herself for a few minutes but she would run into things, maybe even find herself wandering into a place that was dangerous for her.

However, when I attach the leash, I can allow her to explore, but when she begins to stray toward a bad spot, I can make the proper adjustment and our walk is a pleasant experience that ends with our arrival at the appointed destination- home.

Can you relate?

You may not have a blind puppy, but can you relate to the blind spots in your life?

The Gospel of Grace leads us into a life of spiritual freedom. We have a "Born Free" mentality that makes us feel like a whole new world has opened up to us.

However, without the guidance of Truth, we can bump into things, fall down, or even find ourselves wandering into things harmful to us.

Grace didn't get us into those spots, we did.

But we have a guarantee, the Spirit of Truth will guide us into all truth and He will show us the things to come.

That means that the Spirit of Truth will show us:

- **The things we need to avoid**- those things that can cause us harm, physically, emotionally, and spiritually.

- **The things that we need to embrace**- the things in life that move us closer to our destiny.

A proper perspective of the Gospel of Grace isn't an "either/or " perspective, it's a "both/and" perspective.

In the Gospel of Grace balance is required, but it's not a balance of Grace and Law- It is a balance of **Grace and Truth.**

7

The Tie that Binds

We have learned to fly the air like birds and swim the sea like fish, but we have not learned the simple art of living together as brothers. –**Martin Luther King Jr.**

I just celebrated the 5th anniversary of my marriage to the greatest woman on planet earth. Our marriage doesn't consist of drama, arguments, or even as many church people say, "intense fellowship." We have great communication and really understand each other. However, there is one minute thing that causes division in our home. This thorn in our flesh, is none other that- you guessed it- the toilet seat: (Siège detoilette- French translation).

The French translation should have given us every indication that there would be trouble in the house over the toilet.

"Siege-seat." Enough said.

So here is my dilemma.

Early in our marriage I was new to the unsung rules you are just supposed to know. I would go into the restroom and find the toilet seat down. I'm not much of a germaphobe, but I do have to reach down and lift a toilet seat with my hands before using the toilet. I use said toilet, wash my hands, then I remember; "I forgot to put the seat down." But doing so will require me to rewash my hands again, using more soap, and napkins, to put the seat back down. And if I return to the restroom before my wife, I have to go back through the same process again. This created a problem for me: I felt it was unnecessary for me to lift the seat only to let it back down. It made more sense for my wife to simply lift the lid after using, and I would show the same courtesy. Problem Solved.

I had rehearsed this in my mind and was totally prepared to make my case to my wife, and our shared bathroom experience would be wonderful.

But the night before the presentation of my case, my wife got up and went into the bathroom with no lights on. For a few seconds I lay silently praying that I hadn't left the bathroom seat up for my presentation. That prayer went unanswered. After a few seconds of silence the quiet of the house was replaced with the screams of my sleepy wife, who had fallen into the toilet with the seat up.

So after a brief description of her feelings, I realized that my case (as good as it was) was no longer worth the presentation. From that day on, no matter how many times I wash my hands, when I leave the bathroom, the toilet seat is down, and today there is harmony in my house.

It's amazing how such trivial things can cause division in our homes, in our friendships, at our workplace, and in our churches. But don't think this is something new. Our culture celebrates serving **SELF**, and what you like, no matter how it affects others. The problem with that is no matter how able and extraordinary you are, you can only go so far alone. If we need others to help us, then we have to learn to work together in unity and not division.

Henry Ford said, *"Coming together is a beginning. Keeping together is progress. Working together is success."*

As much as we struggle with division in our lives today, we are not the first people, nor will we be the last to deal with this. Paul addresses the Corinthian church which was dealing several acts of division. As we look, try and see if you notice these divisions are more relevant today than many have thought...

1 Corinthians 1:10-12- *"I appeal to you, brothers, by the name of our Lord Jesus Christ, that **all of you agree**, and that there be **no divisions among you**, but **that you be united** in the same mind and the same judgment. ¹¹ For it has been reported to me by Chloe's people that there is quarreling among you, my brothers. ¹² What I mean is that each one of you says, "I follow Paul," or "I follow Apollos," or "I follow Cephas," or "I follow Christ."*

Then his next words... "Is Christ Divided?"

Paul had many issues with the church in Corinth. After greeting them in chapter 1 and giving thanks for them, he jumps right into the issue of division among the ranks.

If you look closely it's a division of preference, not sin.

He says ok, you guys are creating clicks around different preachers...

Some say, "I follow **Paul**" - He is called to minister to the Gentiles. Those people who understood very little about the festivals and traditions of Judaism preferred Paul's ministry over the rest.

Some say, "I follow **Apollos**" - He appeals to the intellectual crowd. He's a tremendous scholar who speaks very eloquently. So the Philosophers, educators, intellectuals are drawn to Apollos's teaching.

Some say, "I follow **Cephas**" - Better known as Peter. Peter probably gets a little crazy with his delivery. But he is also known as a Christian Jew who wants to add the traditions of the Jewish people to Christianity. He's a little Old School. Those who are a bit dogmatic and Old School are probably drawn to Cephas.

Then some say, "I follow **Christ**" - You might be saying this group has it right. We have to remember, Christ has died, resurrected, ascended, and sent the Holy Spirit to establish the church. These people are saying, "I don't have to listen to Paul, Apollos, Peter, or anyone else. I just follow Jesus, I just don't believe I need to submit to a spiritual authority.

Kyle Idleman pointed out this problem in his series *Journey to Deep*. "Preferential Division is grammar school Christianity, and the Apostle Paul addresses the solution in the 3rd chapter of 1 Corinthains: If **Division** is the problem, then **Unity** has to be the solution."

1Corinthians 3:1-11- *"But I, brothers, could not address you as* **spiritual people**, *but* **as people of the flesh, as infants in Christ**.² *I fed you with milk, not solid food, for you were not ready for it. And even now you are not yet ready,* ³ *for you are still of the flesh. For while there is jealousy and strife among you, are you not of the flesh and behaving only in a human way?* ⁴ *For when one says, "I follow Paul," and another, "I follow Apollos," are you not being merely human?*

⁵ *What then is Apollos? What is Paul?* **Servants through whom you believed, as the Lord assigned to each.** ⁶ *I planted, Apollos watered, but* **God gave the growth**. ⁷ *So neither he who plants nor*

he who waters is anything, but only God who gives the growth. ⁸ He who plants and he who waters are one, and each will receive his wages according to his labor. ⁹ For we are God's fellow workers. You are God's field, God's building ¹⁰ **According to the grace** *of God given to me, like a skilled master builder I laid a foundation, and someone else is building upon it. Let each one take care how he builds upon it. ¹¹ For no one can lay a foundation* **other than that which is laid, which is Jesus Christ."**

Notice Paul never says which preference was correct.

We all have different preferences because the Body of Christ is diverse. Different people, different races, different cultures, different social status, different economic status, but God uses a single strand to tie all our differences together. We will then all become God's Building which is built on the foundation of the Cross of Christ.

We are all workers with different gifts to accomplish different tasks working towards a common goal in unity.

What is this tie that binds? Look back at verse 10.

Paul says according to the Grace God has given to me, I am able to do the task He gives me. Grace will empower you to do your task, me to do mine, and the rest of the Body of Christ to do theirs. **Grace is the tie that binds**.

It is what we received to save us and set us on a path of righteousness, and it is the power to accomplish the tasks He gives us to do.

We can have our preferences, because we are wired differently, but we must keep our eyes on the work of Christ and rely on the Power of God's Grace to accomplish our tasks.

United by Grace

Scripture gives some powerful examples of the harm of division as well as the beauty and productiveness of unity. When the children of Israel came out of Egypt, it didn't take long for this united front of God's people to allow division to creep in.

Exodus 19:1- *"On the first day of the third month after the Israelites left Egypt--on that very day--they came to the Desert of Sinai."* (ref. NIV)

If we briefly read over this, it seems like it was 90 days since leaving Egypt that they arrived at Sinai but that is not the case. The scripture says "on that very day". What day? "In the third month . . .on that very day" would mean the first day of the third month. Follow with me...

Israel left Egypt and began their journey on the 15th day of the first month (Exodus Chapter 12).

The fifteenth day of the second month would be 30 days after leaving Egypt. From the 15th of the second month to the end of the month would be another 15 days making a total of 45 days.

The first day of the third month would be the 46th day.

This timeline is important because God came down on Mount Sinai on the 50th day, as we will see in a moment.

When Moses returned from the mountain the first time, and told the children of Israel what God had said they answered, "Whatever God says do, we'll do it." This was the 48th day.

Then on the 50th day since leaving Egypt God came down on the mountain and began speaking. **The 1st Pentecost.**

But when the children of Israel heard God speak...

Exodus 20:18-19- *"Now when all the people saw the thunder and the flashes of lightning and the sound of the trumpet and the mountain smoking, the people were afraid and trembled, and they stood far off ¹⁹ and said to Moses,* **"You speak to us**, *and we will listen; but* **do not let God speak to us**, *lest we die."*

Notice the division. Fear caused God's people to want a middle-man.

So God gave them what they wanted. He called Moses back up the mountain and gave him the Ten Commandments. Remember, they said they would do whatever God said.

While Moses was atop the mountain they got bored and made for themselves a golden calf (an idol to worship.) So when Moses got back down from the mountaintop and saw what was going on, he destroyed the golden calf and asked who would stand with the Lord. Those who stood with the Lord slayed everyone else and on that day 3000 men died. (ref. Exodus 32.)

Here it is in a nutshell.

The people said they would obey whatever God said, but when He spoke, they were afraid and asked for someone to go to God for them (division of disobediance.)

Then while Moses was speaking to God, they made another idol to worship (division of idolotry.)

Then when Moses executed judgment, the nation was divided (division among the ranks) and that divide caused **3000 deaths**!

This all was the beginning of the ***Dispensation of Law***.

Now let us fast forward to another Pentecost. This one from the book of Acts.

Acts 2:1-3- *"When the day of Pentecost arrived,* ***they were all together in one place***. *² And suddenly there came from heaven a* *sound like a mighty rushing wind, and it filled the entire house where they were sitting. ³ And divided tongues as of fire appeared to them and rested on each one of them."*

Jesus had risen and He had promised that the Holy Spirit would come. The people were all together waiting on the same thing.

While they were waiting together (in unity), the promised one came and fell on all them (in unity), and Peter began to preach about Christ and His promise of the Holy Spirit.
The Bible says...

Acts 2:41- *"So those who received his word were baptized, and there were added that day about three thousand souls."*

This was the beginning of the **Dispensation of Grace**.

We see from these examples that rules cause rule breaking, judgmental spirits, pride, and hypocrisy.
However, the power of God's glorious Grace brings unity, and this unity allows us to see ourselves as a small piece of a much bigger picture.
Then, when we acknowledge our insufficiency, we begin to draw from the unending fountain of God's Grace, which provides everything we will ever need.
We have no choice but to love God because He first loved us.
When we love God, we begin to truly love others as ourselves.

GRACE is the tie that binds!!!

8

The Embrace of Grace

Sin does not stop God's grace from flowing, but God's grace will stop sin.
–Joseph Prince

Have you noticed that we Christians sometimes say things that really don't make sense? I have been puzzled by one expression in particular. What exactly are *"travelling mercies?"* Have you ever prayed for *travelling mercies*? I have, but I have no idea why I said those particular words. Sometimes we have people in the car who don't speak Christianeze and if we aren't more sensitive to those around us, we can create more questions for people than answers. So now we make it simple and pray for God's protection (Psalms 91) over trips and we just know that those precious *travelling mercies* are part of the package.

Another thing that I've noticed is that when people share their testimony, they tell of all the destruction and sin from their past and then they throw this in, "And then at such and such time, I FOUND CHRIST, and now my life is better."

I love that, and it is absolutely true except for one thing. They didn't, you didn't, and I didn't FIND CHRIST. **HE FOUND US!**

A perfect picture of this is found in Genesis 3. Adam was given instruction from God how to live life under His protection and blessing, but Adam and Eve didn't follow God's instruction. They sinned. And when they sinned, they didn't start a search party for God to tell Him what happened. They hid.

We do the same thing. We disobey the Word of God. We sin. And when we sin, we hide. So if we are living life in hiding from God, if we are lost, how can we ever say we found Him.

When someone is lost, whether at sea, in the wilderness, on a snow-capped mountain, or in the grocery store, they are in need of rescue. They never say, "Oh I found the rescue team."

No, the rescue team finds them, hence the word RESCUE!

When we are lost, it is clear that we need RESCUE. We long to feel the **Embrace of Grace**. If you are a believer in Christ you have felt that embrace.

But, let me ask you this. If you were lost in an avalanche, or lost at sea, and that hand of Rescue reached out for yours, what would you do? You would latch onto that hand for your very life. Right?

Grace embraces us, and then we have to embrace the Grace! Let me share a story with you.

My entire family is filled with affectionate people, but my sister is extremely affectionate. She's a *hugger*. When we are around larger groups of people, I like to watch my sister interact with the crowd, because Jami is a hugger. But not everyone hugs. I watch my sister embrace people with her genuine affection and the reaction of people, goes one of two ways. The majority of people fall into the first category. They are comfortable with huggers and reciprocate with the same, but some people feel extremely awkward when hugged.

This produces an almost comical scene. It is as if they literally don't know what to do. They aren't mean people; they just do not know how to act under the circumstances. It is funny!

If you are not a hugger, you probably know exactly what I am talking about, but if hugging does not bother you, then you have a hard time understanding why someone simply does not like hugging.

I think a lot of people who are exposed to the message of Grace are the same as non-huggers.

We know the word GRACE. We know GRACE saves us, but when we are drawn into a conversation about GRACE that goes beyond the superficial, we get uncomfortable. We become the awkward non-hugger.

To embrace GRACE, we need to understand **what** we are embracing, **why** we need to embrace GRACE, and **how** we can go about embracing GRACE.

First, we need to know that God gives us scripture to be received in one of two primary ways. Sometimes God's Word is *descriptive* and other times His Word is *prescriptive*.

We can receive the Gospel of Grace when we read the Word as descriptive (meaning God is describing what Grace is) but we can only embrace Grace if we read it as prescriptive (meaning God wants us to put it to work in our lives).

I'll give you an example.

God gives us descriptions of Grace in **John 1:12-17** (previously quoted) and **Ephesians 2:8-9** (previously quoted) telling us how Grace came into the world and that we are saved by Grace.

Then Christ tells us with the story of the Vine and the branches in **John 15:1-11**, what Grace is to the believer.

However, these are descriptive texts that show us how Grace

embraces us so we need to look at some prescriptive texts to see how we can embrace this wonderful Gospel of Grace.

God has created us for more: More than the status quo, more than settling for less.

He has created us for GREATNESS.

Let me show you.

Genesis 1:28-30 - *And God blessed them. And God said to them, "Be fruitful and multiply and fill the earth and subdue it, and have dominion over the fish of the sea and over the birds of the heavens and over every living thing that moves on the earth." 29 And God said, "Behold,* **I have given you** *every plant yielding seed that is on the face of all the earth, and every tree with seed in its fruit. You shall have them for food. 30 And to every beast of the earth and to every bird of the heavens and to everything that creeps on the earth, everything that has the breath of life, I have given every green plant for food."* **And it was so.**

That was what God said to Adam, the first man. That is AWESOME and that cultural mandate was for all mankind, not just Adam – "be fruitful-multiply-take dominion." But what about Adam's fall in the garden, when he disobeyed God's mandate? Didn't that disqualify us? That is a good question. Look at...

Romans 5:18- *"Here it is in a nutshell: Just as one person did it wrong and got us in all this trouble with sin and death, another person did it right and got us out of it. But more than just getting us out of trouble, he got us into life! One man said no to God and put many people in the wrong; one man said yes to God and put many in the right." (ref. MSG)*

Remember GRACE came with Jesus Christ, so GRACE

restored the break in the fall of man. It picked mankind back up and made a way for GREATNESS again.

Not that we are *"all that"*, but the one who lives in us is more than *"all that".*

When we begin to understand Grace, we will no longer be the awkward non-hugger, but we will embrace GRACE and embrace life with a new perspective. We will become huggers.

Here are 3 functions of Grace that will allow us to view the Gospel of Grace both *descriptively* and *prescriptively*.

First, we are saved by Grace (**Eph. 2:4-8**.) This is *descriptive*. We've looked at this several times so far so I'll be brief on it, but we do need to understand that Grace saves us and that Grace is accessed through Faith. Grace must be more than just unmerited favor but the very power of God in Christ that raised Him from the dead. It takes power to take something dead and make it alive. We have all sinned (**Romans 3:23**) and the wages/payment of sin is death, but the gift of God/Grace is eternal life (**Romans 6:23**.) Grace takes us from death to life- that's power. We access that power through the conduit of Faith. When we place our hope in Christ for a new life, a life of GREATNESS, and we place that trust in Christ, we access the power of the resurrection in our lives.

Second, Grace is the power to live in Holiness. This is *prescriptive.*

Romans 5:17- *"For if, because of one man's trespass, death reigned through that one man, much more will* **those who receive the abundance of grace** *and the free gift of righteousness reign in life through the one man Jesus Christ."*

We can reign in life through Christ. But Adam sinned, what about me? Won't I just mess it all up for everyone else?

Romans 6:14- *"For sin will have no dominion over you, since you are not under law but under grace."*

You have changed. You have become a new person (**2 Corinthians 5:17.**)

Alexander the Great, one of the greatest military generals who ever lived, conquered almost the entire known world with his vast army. One night during a campaign, he couldn't sleep and left his tent to walk around the campgrounds. As he was walking he came across a soldier asleep on guard duty – a serious offense. The penalty for falling asleep on guard duty was, in some cases, instant death; the commanding officer sometimes poured oil on the sleeping soldier and lit it. The soldier began to wake up as Alexander approached him. Recognizing who was standing in front of him, the young man feared for his life. "Do you know what the penalty is for falling asleep on guard duty?" Alexander the Great asked the soldier. "Yes, sir," the soldier responded in a quivering voice.

"Soldier, what's your name?" demanded Alexander the Great.

"Alexander, sir." Alexander the Great repeated the question: "What is your name?"

"My name is Alexander, sir," the soldier repeated.

A third time and more loudly Alexander the Great asked, "What is your name?"

A third time the soldier meekly said, "My name is Alexander, sir."

Alexander the Great then looked the young soldier straight in the eye. "Soldier," he said with intensity, "either change your name or change your conduct." (source unknown /snopes.com)

There is a great lesson in this story. When Grace has made us new, we change. It's that simple. Sin still tugs at our coattail but it has no dominion over us.

Grace is not something to be taken advantage of, or abused by us.

It gives us the "WANT TO" live a better life- to live in the GREATNESS God created us for.

And ***third***, Grace is in our lives to further the Kingdom of God here on earth. This is also *prescriptive*.

Romans 1:5- *"through whom we have received grace and apostleship to bring about the obedience of faith for the sake of his name among all the nations."*

Grace is the power to take the message of the Gospel to all nations just as Christ commanded in **Matthew 28:19**. When that power flows, lives are changed. And when lives are changed, the world is changed.

Acts 17:6- *"These men who have turned the world upside down..."*

These guys that turned the world upside down were not biblical scholars that had been approved by a denominational or church executive board. They were normal men (**Acts 4:13**.) When they embraced Grace, when they began to see Grace as prescriptive, the message of the Gospel began to explode throughout the area, and later throughout the world. Let's look at a few examples...

Peter (one of these ordinary men) preached an extraordinary sermon on Pentecost and the Kingdom grew.

Acts 2:41- *"So those who received his word were baptized, and there were added that day about* **three thousand souls.***"*

Those believers began to meet together and meet the needs of the community. They had generous hearts and...

Acts 2:47- *"...praising God and having favor with all the people.* ***And the Lord added to their number day by day*** *those who were being saved."*

And as the number of believers increased, so did the number of those sharing the Gospel of Grace with others.

Acts 6:7-*"And the word of God continued to increase,* ***and the number of the disciples multiplied greatly*** *in Jerusalem, and a great many of the priests became obedient to the faith."*

Grace embraces us and we are radically saved. Then the regenerate heart in us embraces the Grace and we not only have the power to live a holy life but we become conduits for the power of the resurrection of Christ. That power changes the world.

Acts 4:33- *"And with great power the apostles gave witness to the resurrection of the Lord Jesus,* ***and great grace was upon them all.****"*

That is how it worked with the early church, and that is how it works **NOW** for those who believe.

Rhythms of Grace

Experiencing the rhythmic flow of the Gospel

Part III

Living the Gospel of Grace

9

The Cadence of Grace

If a man does not keep pace with his companions, perhaps it is because he hears a different drummer. Let him step to the music, which he hears, however measured or far away- **Henry David Thoreau**

I have always been fascinated with the military. In the 9th grade my parents let me go to Military School (I know what you're thinking, sure they LET you go.) But really I wanted to go. I wanted to be Rambo, so I went to Military School to learn how to become just like Rambo.

One of the most memorable things about that year was when we would march or run. Early in the morning we would begin the day with a 2 mile run, then we would march everywhere we went. The running and walking weren't my favorite things, but rather what we did as we walked and ran. You see, while we were marching or running we were singing CADENCES.

Left. Left. Left, Right, Left!

1, 2, 3, 4

1, 2, 3, 4

1, 2.... 3, 4!

I was fascinated with the sound, the feel, and the influence of it all. I loved to sing cadence. But only recently did I learn the purpose of those cadences and I was inspired.

The origins of cadences are rooted in music but as soldiers began to use them in formations, they served a much greater purpose.

The cadence call moves to the beat and rhythm but it also serves the purpose of keeping the unit in step and in formation. It serves to build teamwork, to cause the unit to remember moments of tragedy and victory all at the same time. It takes the mind off one's self and places it on the movement of the unit. A unit can move further faster, has higher self-esteem, and is much more unified and effective as a result of singing cadences.

That is what the church needs today: we need a cadence to which we can march to.

We need a cadence that will cause us to stay in step; in step with the Spirit of God, and in step with each other.

1 John 1:7- *"But if we walk in the light, as he is in the light, we have **fellowship with one another**, and the blood of Jesus, his Son, purifies us from all sin."*

We need a cadence that will call us to be in formation. When believers are in unity, it is a beautiful thing.

Psalm 133:1- *"Behold, how **good and pleasant** it is **when brothers dwell in unity.**"*

We need a cadence that prompts a call and response dialogue signifying communication and encouragement to one another in love.

We need each other in our daily lives and nothing leads to that more than the "Cadence of Grace."

This does not mean that everyone will walk to the same beat. That never seems to happen. But as believers we must all march under the same banner, the banner of Christ.

There will be some people who walk in cadence with you for a season, and then there are those who will do so for life.

The important thing to remember is that just because someone is not in step with you does not mean they are against you. They are just marching to a different beat, or are in a different season of life. You march to the beat you hear.

When you walk in your purpose, you will notice some people come along side you and begin marching to the same beat, and others will walk away.

Embrace those who come along side. They are your team.

You will share victories, you will share loss, but most of all, you will share the *Cadence of Grace.*

Early in the Bible we see a great story of the Cadence of Grace. Let's look…

Starting in **Judges chapter 6** we see the nation of Israel being oppressed by Midian. Israel had moved into the mountains and began hiding in caves from the Midianites. It was so oppressive that when it came time for Israel to harvest a crop, the Midianites would come and steal the crop from them. It was bad!

But one day God sent for a man named Gideon. The angel of the Lord told Gideon that he was to be used to set the Israelites free from oppression. Gideon had a hard time believing this, but reluctantly agreed to try. So he rounded up a small group of 22,000 people for the task.

Some people look at Gideon like a scared puppy, but anyone who can rally 22,000 people for a task is a pretty strong leader.

But God wasn't on board with using 22,000 people. He didn't want any misplaced credit for this accomplishment, so He trimmed the crowd down to 10,000.

Now we must note that the Midianites had an army of around 135,000 (according to **Judges 8:10**,) so Gideon had his hands full already fighting with only 22,000. He must have been freaking out when God trimmed it to 10,000. But God wasn't finished yet.

God told Gideon to give one final test to the soldiers. And when this final test was over there were only 300 left. So just to make sure we are on the same page...

Midian had 135,000 soldiers

Israel started with 22,000 (too many)

God trimmed the number down to 10,000 (still too many)

Now it's 135,000 Midianites vs. 300 Israelites

But that's not all.

Then the Lord tells Gideon the weapons he is to take into battle.

Swords? Nope. Sheilds? Nope.

So what does God tell him to take?

Trumpets, torches and clay pots!

I know. I thought the same thing. But this is where the Cadence of Grace comes into play.

When those 300 men gathered together, God began a call and response dialogue that would bring freedom to the entire nation of Israel.

If you can only imagine these men readying themselves for battle, moving into ranks and coming to attention. About this time God begins the cadence.

"Company, ATTENTION!"

" Forward MARCH."

 Left, Left, Left, Right, Left. 1, 2, 3, 4 ⁻ 1, 2, 3, 4 ⁻ 1, 2, 3,4 ⁻ 1, 2….3, 4!

The Cadence of Grace is infectious. God's passion became

their passion and nothing seemed impossible anymore. They moved into position on the battlefield and here is what happens...

Judges 7:19-23- *"So Gideon and the hundred men who were with him came to the outskirts of the camp at the beginning of the middle watch, when they had just set the watch. And they blew the trumpets and smashed the jars that were in their hands.* [20] ***Then the three companies blew the trumpets and broke the jars.*** *They held in their left hands the torches, and in their right hands the trumpets to blow. And they cried out, "A sword for the LORD and for Gideon!"* [21] ***Every man stood in his place*** *around the camp, and all the army ran. They cried out and fled.* [22] ***When they blew the 300 trumpets, the LORD set every man's sword against his comrade and against all the army.*** *And the army fled as far as Beth-shittah toward Zererah, as far as the border of Abel-meholah, by Tabbath.* [23] *And the men of Israel were called out from Naphtali and from Asher and from all Manasseh,* ***and they pursued after Midian.****"*

The story goes on to say that Gideon's army chases down the two princes of Midian. The tables have turned and no longer is the nation of Israel hiding, but their enemies are on the run, and hiding.

Gideon didn't do anything to earn such favor in the eyes of the Lord. Nor did the nation of Israel.

This was a supernatural act of God's Grace. It was undeserved, yet it was given to them.

As God's instruction came to Gideon, the Rhythms of Grace began to sound off like a cadence to those 300 men. They were in formation, and unity. God's instruction and teamwork became their cadence, and victory was the result. They walked in step and when the time came they all responded with a sound of Victory together.

Not many of us would say we've seen this kind of story flesh itself out in our lives, but if you think about it, perhaps we have.

Every time we rally around a response to social injustice, we become part of something bigger, greater. This could be as simple as giving a bag of groceries to a family in need or helping a community devastated by a natural disaster. You may be called to help someone struggling with addiction, to make a change in their lives, or adopting an orphan.

No matter what the situation is, when you rally around the needs of "the least of these", you have the opportunity to get in step with the Cadence of Grace and make a difference in your world. That is what Gideon did and that is what we can all do. However that fleshes itself out in your life, make sure to guard against thinking you are awesome for doing what you do. Look at how Gideon responded to this...

Judges 7:22-23- *"Then the men of Israel said to Gideon, "Rule over us, you and your son and your grandson also, for you have saved us from the hand of Midian." 23 Gideon said to them,* ***"I will not rule over you****, and my son will not rule over you;* ***the LORD will rule over you.****"*

Gideon did not lose sight of Grace. He knew that God created the Cadence. God made the way, and in it all, God alone deserved the Glory. The Cadence of Grace always has God leading the charge.

The Cadence of Grace is very simple when it relates to us. We have three primary responsibilities.

1. **LISTEN**- our first response is to listen to what God says, and

hear the cadence.

> **Deuteronomy 32:1-2-** *"Give ear, O heavens, and I will speak, and let the earth hear the words of my mouth.2 May my teaching drop as the rain, my speech distill as the dew, like gentle rain upon the tender grass, and like showers upon the herb."*

2. **FOLLOW-** then we must act on what we hear. We must get in step and follow with the cadence.

> **Matthew 16:24-** *"Then Jesus told his disciples, "If anyone would come after me, let him deny himself and take up his cross and follow me."*

3. **OBEY-** finally we must obey the instructive rhythm of the cadence. This is where the supernatural happens.

> **Deuteronomy 28:1-** *"And if you faithfully obey the voice of the LORD your God, being careful to do all his commandments that I command you today, the LORD your God will set you high above all the nations of the earth."*

Scripture states that if we obey, then everything we touch will be blessed.

Everywhere we go will be blessed.

We will live a blessed life.

Our lives will be in sync with the will of God, and there is no greater joy than being in sync with God's will. But remember the Cadence of Grace does not mean we will live perfect lives. It simply means we trust one that is absolutely perfect with our lives.

The *Cadence of Grace* calls each of us out of our comfort zone and calls us into His purpose, whatever that looks like in our individual lives.

It moves us to a place none of us deserves to be, but to which all of us can go when we give our lives totally to the mission and call of God.

When we **LISTEN**, **FOLLOW**, and **OBEY** the Cadence of God's Grace, we begin to truly experience the life God created us for.

Now is the time to act.

God has declared a purpose for your life. What are you going to do with this information?

Many people have been taught this, but have never let this revelation move them to action . Let me ask you this:

What injustice do you want to see made right?

What is it that tugs at your heart in our world?

What keeps you awake at night?

What passion wakes you up early in the morning?

If you could do anything to make a change in the world, what would that be?

God placed that passion in your heart for **His** purpose. And here is the good news...

YOU CAN'T FAIL!

Oh, you might fail at *your task*, but never at *HIS*.

God has a perfect record at *NEVER FAILING!*

So what are you waiting on?

The Cadence of Grace is calling out to you right now.

What are you going do about it?

Be encouraged by the words of the author of the book of Hebrews...

Hebrews 6:10 – *"God is not unjust; he will not forget your work and the love you have shown him as you have helped his people and continue to help them."*

10

No More Blurred Lines

The successful man is the average man, focused. –**Unknown**

As I said in an earlier chapter, I have a past filled with bad decisions, drugs and alcohol, prison, and many broken relationships. You could call me a slow learner, but it wasn't until my 30's that I began to really seek to make a change.

After much seeking, I found the only person that could put everything back together again.

His name is Jesus and this is how I came to know Him.

After spending four years in prison, I heard the greatest news a prisoner ever hears. "You are being released."

I had made up my mind; this time was going to be different. So, I took a bus to a recovery program facility. I got a job, was staying clean, life was good.

About six months into this new life I began to use drugs again, and in a couple of months things were as bad as they had ever been.

All the plans of a better life were being shot up my arm every day. I won't bore you with all the depraved details, but a good thing soon turned to bad, and eventually bad decisions took me full circle and once again I went to jail.

After three months I was released in the middle of the night

150 miles from the place I called "home." Nobody would take my calls, or send me money to get home.

I only had an address of a Christian Recovery program.

I began walking.

I walked across town to the location of the program. I arrived only to find out they didn't have an available bed. But they did give me the number of another rehabilitation program about 25 miles further from home. Not closer to home, but further away.

I called and this is where it gets really strange. When I talked with the founder of the program, he was clear that it wasn't a program, but a ministry. He also said he'd send someone for me right away.

This man's name is Pastor Waymon Johnson, founder of New Birth Ministries, and this one man was the catalyst to my understanding of the Gospel of Grace.

The next morning Pastor Johnson sent the director of the ministry to pick me up. The wait for these guys was an incredibly anxious time for me. My body was begging for any type of drug or alcohol, my mind was contemplating what the catch was going to be (what kind of financial commitment they were going to need), but my spirit was crying out for a change.

God was on a search and rescue mission- the target- **yours truly**. I saw immediately that this place was going to be different.

Here are a few things that stuck out…

They told me not to worry about any intake fees. Money wasn't what they wanted. They said God provided for the needs of the ministry. If a resident had the intake fee-fine, but if not; that was fine too. This blew me away.

They gave me clothes. When I arrived, I only had the

clothes that I was wearing. They took me to get plenty of clothing to last me a couple of weeks. Again, no strings attached. I had no money so they provided for everything.

They didn't expect me to be perfect. Though they were strong Christians, they knew I wasn't and they knew it would be a process for me, a spiritual journey that would take time.

They had patience with my immaturity and it was not until much later that I understood why.

Let me go back and walk you through how these acts of kindness began a process that would forever change my life. The acts of kindness didn't fix the problem, but it started a process that fixed the problem.

I have had help from other people my entire life, but I had never had help without strings attached. Everyone wants something from you, so when you receive help from someone, you know that they expect something in return- you owe them. But Pastor Waymon Johnson didn't want anything from me. He wanted change for my life, and he was prepared to help me change.

They took me in with no expectations of what I would bring to the table. Grace does the same thing.

Philip Yancey, in his book "*What's So Amazing About Grace,*" touches on what makes Christianity different from other world religions.

"During a British conference on comparative religions, experts from around the world debated what, if any, belief was unique to the Christian faith. They began by eliminating possibilities. Incarnation? Other religions had different versions of gods appearing in human form. Resurrection? Again, other religions had accounts of return from death. The debate went on for some time until C.S. Lewis wandered into the room.

"What's the rumpus about?" he asked, and heard in reply that his colleagues were discussing Christianity's unique contribution among world religions. Lewis responded, "Oh, that's easy. It's Grace." *(Grand Rapids, Michigan: Zondervan Publishing House, 1997, p. 45)*

Grace gave me access to the favor of God (something I didn't deserve.) This was unlike anything I had ever experienced.

The walls of cynicism I had built around my life came crashing down by a single act of kindness from someone else, and that opened my heart to receive the Gospel of Grace offered me through Christ Jesus.

If you think everything has a string attached to it, or you think the only reasons people are kind to one another involve selfish motives, I want to tell you this is not the case. Yes, there are many enslaved by their selfishness, but there are also people who are agents of Grace assigned to your life, to your situation. When the real thing touches you, life will never be the same.

That is how it happened for me, and it happened in a way that only God could have arranged.

The fact that New Birth provided me with clothing taught me that I could trust God for provision in my life. I did not have to beg or even ask for the things I needed.

God knew what I needed at that time and He used other people to provide what I needed. Again, this was something completely foreign to me. But later I saw that this was not a one-direction blessing. God provided for me in a time of need, and then later He would use me to bless others in the same fashion.

God will provide what you need, but you are *blessed*... to be a *blessing*.

If you think the blessings of God travel in one direction (to you) then you have missed the point of the Gospel of Grace.

We receive freely (GRACE), but we also should give freely (GRACE.) We aren't effective ambassadors of Grace if we only allow blessings to flow one way.

The most important lesson about Grace I learned through the ministry of Pastor Waymon Johnson and New Birth Ministries was that they didn't expect me to be perfect. When I arrived at New Birth Ministries, I had no intention of living for Christ. My intention was to stop using drugs for long enough that I could maintain a normal life without the need for substances, then I would move back home and continue life as usual, without drugs.

I was a smoker, which was against the rules of the program, and would become a major roadblock to my recovery. But these guys didn't expect me to have all these issues worked out as soon as I got there. They were patient with me and my issues. They trusted the God that changed their lives, to do the same with me.

This is where the lines get blurry at times in the church. It is so easy to trust God to save people, but once they choose to follow Christ, many times we feel it is our *responsibility* to make sure they grow into the person God created them to be. Let me be crystal clear. The church does have *responsibility* in the life of a believer; but we are tasked with making disciples, as witnesses, but **NOT** to be judge and jury. If someone is saved according to scripture, the Holy Spirit lives in that person. That means the same teacher, comforter, and counsellor that is constantly revealing Christ to us, is doing the same work in the life of ALL new believers.

Sometimes our intention to reveal the way of Christ to a new believer becomes more of a roadblock than a pathway. We don't have the power to change people. We simply can't do it.

But thankfully Grace does the work that we can't do.

That is what I experienced when I came to Christ. I believe the reason such incredible change happened in my life is because I was surrounded by people who were aware I was not perfect, and did not expect me to be. They realized God was perfectly capable of bringing about change in me, and that would come in His time.

They realized Grace could change me and shape me into the image of Christ. Grace always brings freedom not bondage.

Trying to force people to be better followers of Christ will always result in a works mentality and rob the power of Grace that is at work in their life.

We try to protect new believers from sin, but Grace is perfectly capable of doing that.

The apostle Paul puts it this way...

Romans 6:14- *"For sin will have no dominion over you, since* ***you are not under law but under grace.***"

Our responsibility is simply to point the new believer to their deep need for fellowship with the Holy Spirit. He will point them to Christ. That is the way discipleship happens, and that is the way Jesus said it would happen.

John 15:26- *"But when the Helper comes, whom I will send to you from the Father, the Spirit of truth, who proceeds from the Father, he will bear witness about me."*

Fellowship with the Holy Spirit reveals Christ to us, full of Grace and Truth.

Christ saves us.

Christ sanctifies us.

We, as believers have the honor of being witnesses of this truth. Our obligation is to share that with the world and let Christ do the work in their hearts.

When the guilt in my heart was heaviest and exposed for all to see, Grace was there.

I began to see through the life of Pastor Waymon Johnson what the heartbeat of God was towards humanity.

When the guilt of sin was heaviest, God sent His only Son to give His life for payment for that sin.

It is important to know that God's Son was perfect (without sin) when He became the payment for our sin.

2 Corinthians 5:21- *"For our sake he made him to be sin who knew no sin, so that in him we might become the righteousness of God."*

Jesus was deserving of blessing and honor because He lived a life of righteousness. We, on the other hand, deserved the wrath of God because of our unrighteousness (our sin.) But for our sake, Jesus switched places with us. He took the punishment for our sins and granted us all the blessings of God that He alone deserved.

That is Grace.

Grace is something that is completely undeserved, so it can only be experienced when we acknowledge we are undeserving.

I didn't deserve a second chance, but God made it possible for me to meet Waymon Johnson who showed me a tangible example of what God made available to me through faith.

I became a recipient of the Gospel of Grace.

Where the law says, "Do better,"

Grace says, "You are better."

The law makes it clear what it stands against, but Grace defines itself by what it stands for.

To state is simply, Grace is love in action.

It is God's passionate unfailing love for us expressed when we didn't deserve it at all.

Romans 11:6- *"But if it is by grace, it is no longer on the basis of works; otherwise grace would no longer be grace."*

If we try to add to Grace, or take away from Grace, it is no longer Grace but something we have created ourselves.

It is hard to imagine this gift of God being that simple, but it is! You can try your best to live a life pleasing to God, and it won't make you any more righteous. It will create a more intimate relationship with Christ, but it won't make you more righteous.

Your righteousness has nothing to do with who you are, or what you do. It has everything to do with what Christ did and who He is.

According to **Ephesians 2:8**, it is Grace that saves you through faith in Christ.

It is a gift. It isn't a result of anything you've done, but what Christ did. This keeps pride from becoming an issue in the Gospel of Grace.

When we begin to live life through these lenses, the lines become clear. It is Christ centered, and we are the undeserving recipients of His wonderful Grace.

There is nothing blurry about that.

When we see life in that way our vision becomes crystal clear.

We begin to be agents of that Gospel of Grace, and we live every moment to the praise of His Glorious Grace.

11

YOLO

Our truest life is when we are in dreams awake. - **Henry David Thoreau**

One of the most frequently asked, yet least understood questions is, "What should I do with my life?" We search constantly for our purpose.

We begin by focusing on our talents and interests.

That is a great place to start, but there is some groundwork to be established first. Before knowing what we should do with our life, shouldn't we first determine, "What is my life?"

In many circumstances, we try and and answer this question by engaging others in small talk.

On a plane, in a barbershop/hair salon, or a doctor's waiting room, you find yourself in a conversation with the person in the seat next to you and after some general chit-chat one of you will ask the magic question- "What do you do for a living?" Why is this always an ice-breaker question? It is a concern because the heart of mankind longs to answer the question, "What is my life?" But there are two problems with turning to others in seeking your purpose.

First, how can *I* answer the question, "What is my life?" by asking what someone else does with *theirs*? This is a problem of displaced identity. There is a reason God only made one you. He has a purpose destined for you, and a personality custom-made for you, so don't try to be someone else. That person is already taken.

The *second* problem is, we seek to receive some type of affirmation or guidance from others, as to how my life should look.

Both situations have us seeking externally for answers to a very internal question,

"What is my life?"

If we are able to answer this question in proper context, then the question of our life's direction will answer itself. No matter where you are from, what your background is, your education, or your occupation, God's Grace brings definition to your life. Grace says…

You are God's child. The creator of the heavens and the earth calls you son or daughter.

John 1:12- *"But to all who did receive him, who believed in his name, he gave the right to become* **children of God.**"

You are justified and redeemed. Your past doesn't define you. A new life is available today through Christ.

Romans 3:24- *"and are* ***justified*** *by his grace as a gift, through the* ***redemption*** *that is in Christ Jesus."*

You have become the righteousness of God in Christ.

2 Corinthians 5:21- *"For our sake he made him to be sin who knew no sin, so that in him* **we might become the righteousness of God.**"

You are made for unity with other Christ followers.

Galatians 3:28- *"There is neither Jew nor Greek, there is neither slave nor free, there is no male and female, for **you are all one in Christ Jesus.**"*

God's Grace makes it all possible.

Ephesians 1:7- *"In him we have redemption through his blood, the forgiveness of our trespasses, **according to the riches of his grace,**"*

The richness of God's Grace is given to restore our lives back to relationship with Him and to give true definition to the lives we were created to live.

A few years before we met, my wife, Meg had the opportunity to fly with **The Blue Angels** (my wife is pretty cool.)

As much as I would like to share all the details of this experience with you, I want to focus on one particular moment that happened pre-flight.

Before climbing into the jet for one of life's bucket list moments, a video crew met with my wife and her parents on the tarmac. They asked a few questions about what this event meant to each of them.

Meg was simply ecstatic! Her parents, Susie and Mike, were excited but a little worried (as anyone would be), but Mike's response, was one I will never forget.

He said, "There are three extremely significant days in any person's life. These are the day you are born, the day you are born again, and TODAY!"

That day proved to be a very significant day for my wife, but that wasn't the last one.

She was involved in disaster relief efforts after hurricane Katrina, worked with some of the greatest people on the planet in ministry, seen countless people make the decision to follow Christ, and the most significant of all, she met and married me (much more to my benefit than hers,) but I digress.

She took Mike's words to heart, and I take them to heart as well.

Let's walk through his statement and see how it relates to each and every one of us.

1st SIGNIFICANT DAY (the day we are born)- I can't remember the day I was born, but I know it was a significant day for my parents, because the day my son Dakota was born is one I will never forget. The miracle of new life is something you will always remember no matter what your belief system; but when you see it through the eyes of a believer in Christ, you gain a new perspective of Christ's love and the price of the Gospel.

God gave His only son because He loved us, so we wouldn't perish, but would have eternal life in fellowship with Him.

The birth of the human body points to a creator and to the Grace of that creator.

Genesis 2:7- "*then the LORD God formed the man of dust from the ground and breathed into his nostrils the breath of life, and the man became a living creature.*"

When we woke up this morning and made our way to the *much-coveted* coffee maker to begin another day, our body had to carry out thousands of interconnected and complicated impulses that we are unaware of, or take for granted. Blood has to course through our veins, oxygen has to be pumped into our lungs, muscles exerted and stretched, just to get us out of bed. Our body is an amazing thing. The average human brain has close to 100 billion neurons that send impulses at up to 268 mph.

The average heart pumps 48 million gallons of blood in a lifetime, which travels over 12,000 miles through the body each day.

Each one of us has breathed over 20,000 times in the last 24 hours. (ref. Discovery Health)

There isn't any doubt in my mind that this incredible creation points to a creator, and just pondering the wonder of our bodies makes our birth a very significant day!

2nd SIGNIFICANT DAY (the day we are born again)- The day of our birth is very significant, but despite the marvel and complexity of human life, every one of us is born with a flaw.

Sure, some people are born with a super genetic makeup; some have an inherent edge intellectually, and some have all the resources available to provide a clear advantage, but we all are born with the same flaw.

We are all born with a sin-nature.

Psalms 51:5- *"Surely I was sinful at birth, sinful from the time my mother conceived me."* (ref. NIV)

The good news is it doesn't have to be a permanent condition. Grace offers a new life.

Romans 5:17- *"For if, because of one man's trespass, death reigned through that one man, much more will those who receive the abundance of grace and the free gift of righteousness reign in life through the one man Jesus Christ."*

Grace fixes the flaw we were born with.
Grace repairs the breach that sin caused.
When we ask Christ into our hearts everything changes.
We become a new creation.

2 Corinthians 5:17- *"Therefore, if anyone is in Christ,* ***he is a new creation.*** *The old has passed away; behold, the new has come."*

When we begin a life in Christ we become a different person, a new person. Just as a butterfly can never be a caterpillar again, we can never be the person we used to be. Our flesh may tell us we are still the same old person, but our spirit is a new creation, and life will never be the same. From this moment on, God wants to use this new creation for ministry.

2 Corinthians 5:18-20 - *"**All this is from God,** who through Christ reconciled us to himself and **gave us the ministry of reconciliation**; that is, in Christ God was reconciling the world to himself, not counting their trespasses against them, and **entrusting to us the message of reconciliation**. Therefore, we are ambassadors for Christ, God **making his appeal through us.** We implore you on behalf of Christ, be reconciled to God."*

We are made new and given the message of the Gospel to share with the world we live in. We are part of God's design to reconcile people to Himself, just like He did in us. What an honor to be trusted with such an important task. We are ambassadors for Christ!

We are given all the authority of the office of an ambassador as well as all the responsibility. We represent the savior of the world. Rest assured though, Christ takes every step with us.

We aren't just in good hands; we are in God's hands.

This cannot happen by merely changing us. Change is good, but change is not what Christ does by Grace.

It is actually an EXCHANGE that takes place.

2 Corinthians 5:21- *"For our sake he made him to be sin who knew no sin, so that in him we might become the righteousness of God."*

We were destined to receive the wrath of God for our sin, our idolatry, and our selfishness.

Christ lived a life of total righteousness. He walked according to the law without sin. He was deserving of all the blessings and honor of God.

Instead of God pouring out His wrath on us for all we deserved, Christ basically switched places with us. He made an exchange on the cross. In this exchange, Christ stepped into our spot and took all the wrath of God in His body for the sin of mankind; past, present, and future.

We stepped into Christ's spot, and in the exchange, we became eligible for all the blessings of God.

Everything Christ deserved became ours. He took all we deserved in order to save us.

It wasn't just change that happened, but literally an exchange.

That is Good News. That is GRACE.

This is called "The Great Exchange". God's love poured out onto us when we didn't deserve it, and Christ taking our sin when He didn't deserve it.

So when God looks at us He isn't seeing our past, our failures, or our shortcomings. He is seeing His son, who exchanged places with us.

3rd SIGNIFICANT DAY (Today)- Today could be the most significant day of your life. The sad thing is, many of us can't enjoy today because we are so mindful of yesterday or tomorrow.

We all have residue from our past that tries to steal the joy of today, but Christ has made us new. The old me is gone, and if I'm ever going to have a better tomorrow, I'm going to have to make the most of today.

How can I do that?

It's easy. Grace!

God didn't send His son to the cross to place us under the bondage of do's and don'ts.

He came to give us life. As Christians, our lives should be that of an MVP player on the football field, not a referee running up and down the field blowing a whistle at other peoples mistakes.

If you aren't a big fan of the message of Grace, you are playing the role of the *referee*, wasting valuable time pointing out others flaws when God needs *you* in the game.

Today is a gift.

We have today to love our spouse, love our children, and love those in our community, even to love our enemies (as hard as it may be.) But most of all we have been given this gift to LIVE.

John 10:10b- "*...I came so they can have **real and eternal life, more and better life than they ever dreamed of**.*" (ref. MSG)

I want that kind of life.

When God tells you He's going to give you an abundant life, you can bank on it. Your prayers and mine need to be, "God show me how to honor You with what You've given me."

I'm not talking about "stuff," I'm talking about what really matters to the heart of God.

PEOPLE.

People matter to God, so people should matter to you and to me. But that abundant life comes with abundant challenges (tests even.)

Rick Warren said this in A <u>Purpose Driven Life</u>. (PDL ch. 16) *"Knowing that one day you will stand before God, here are some questions you need to consider: How will you explain those times when projects or things were more important to you than people? Who do you need to start spending more time with? What do you need to cut out of your schedule to make that possible? What sacrifices do you need to make?*

"The best use of life is love. The best expression of love is time. The best time to love is now."

So back to the title of this chapter, "YOLO".
Many people know what this means, but for the sake of those who don't, it means-**You Only Live Once.**

It is a form of "text" or social media language like shorthand, to communicate more efficiently or in code. Last week my wife was telling a story to her grandparents and during the story her mom looked at her and in the sweetest voice said, "TMI".

I almost died laughing hearing this.

> **TMI**- *Too much information.*
> **SMH**-*Shaking my head.*
> **RME**- *Rolling my eyes.*
> **LOL**- *Laughing out loud.*
> and the mighty **YOLO**.

It's true you only live once, but in Christ you get a second chance at that one life.
That's Amazing!
That's Grace!!
That's AMAZING GRACE!!!

12

Bethany, will you say Grace?

"How many things have to happen to you before something occurs to you?"
–**Robert Frost**

One of my favorite movies of all time is National Lampoon's Christmas Vacation. Every year we gather a group of friends and family to watch this seasonal classic.

My wife and I constantly make reference to lines from the movie because it's so felicitous. As with any great movie, we all have our favorite scene. Here is mine.

After all the family gathers for the annual Griswold Christmas at Clark's home, the family sits down to a wonderful Christmas meal. At this point, Clark stands up and addresses the family.

Clark- "Since this is Aunt Bethany's 80th Christmas, I think she should lead us in the saying of grace."
Aunt Bethany- "What dear?"
Uncle Louis (Bethany's husband)- "Grace."
Aunt Bethany- "Grace? (pause) She passed away 30 years ago."
Uncle Louis- "They want you to say grace. (pause) The blessing."

At this point Aunt Bethany seems to understand and proceeds to say the *"Pledge of Allegiance."*

If you've never seen this scene, it is priceless, but I feel as if many people are just like Aunt Bethany in their understanding of Grace.

We talk about Grace, believe in Grace, but when we are called upon to explain it, it's like we completely miss the point.

We dance around the topic, we do the whole spin-doctor thing in our explanation, when the world needs us to "say Grace."

If you are a believer in Christ, then you are an object of Grace; but you aren't just an object of Grace, but also an instrument of Grace. There is a really special story in the Gospel of John that is a picture of this very thing.

Peter finds himself weighted down with self-condemnation after he denied Christ (just as Jesus said he would.)

Christ has been crucified and Peter feels lost.

Then Peter hears of the resurrection of Christ, but he still hasn't had THE conversation with Jesus about his denial.

So, what does Peter do?

Just like any good southern boy he goes fishing.

After fishing on the sea of Tiberias all night, with no luck, the disciples encounter a stranger on the banks. He tells them to cast their nets on the right side of the boat.

The result was an overload of fish.

John recognizes the stranger as Jesus, and before they can get the boat turned around, Peter jumps in the water and swims for shore.

Some say Peter did this to avoid being chastised in front of his friends, but either way, a time for THE talk had presented itself.
The story picks up in...

John 21:8 – "*8 The other disciples came in the boat, dragging the net full of fish, for they were not far from the land, but about a hundred yards off. 9 When they got out on land, they saw a charcoal fire in place, with fish laid out on it, and bread. 10 Jesus said to them, "Bring some of the fish that you have just caught." 11 So Simon Peter went aboard and hauled the net ashore, full of large fish, 153 of them, and although there were so many, the net was not torn. 12 Jesus said to them, "**Come and have breakfast.**" Now none of the disciples dared ask him, "Who are you?" They knew it was the Lord. 13 Jesus came and took the bread and gave it to them, and so with the fish. 14 **This was now the third time that Jesus was revealed to the disciples after he was raised from the dead.***

I want to point out a couple of things here:

Peter has always been a really confrontational guy. He chopped a guys ear off to try and protect Jesus, but when things got rough, he denied Him. One would think that he would prompt a disscussion about why he denied Jesus, but he didn't. So Peter isn't as confrontational as we've always thought, but he must have wanted to get this off his chest.

First, Jesus says, "Come and have breakfast."
After Peter jumped out of the boat and swam to shore, Jesus wants to eat (verse 12.) This had to be torture for Peter, but then we get another picture of how bad this had to be bothering Peter in verse 14.

This was the third time Jesus had revealed Himself to the disciples after the resurrection.

First Corinthians 15 even says Jesus appeared to Peter before
the others but they still haven't had THE talk.

Surely Peter is anxious.

Finally, the time arrives in verse 15.

John 21:15- "*¹⁵ When they had finished breakfast, Jesus said to Simon Peter,*
"Simon, son of John, do you love me more than these?"

He said to him, "Yes, Lord; you know that I love you."

He said to him, "Feed my lambs."

¹⁶ He said to him a second time, "Simon, son of John, do you love me?"

He said to him, "Yes, Lord; you know that I love you."

He said to him, "Tend my sheep."

¹⁷ He said to him the third time, "Simon, son of John, do you love me?"

Peter was grieved because he said to him the third time, "Do you love me?" and he said to him, "Lord, you know everything; you know that I love you."

Jesus said to him, "Feed my sheep.

Peter had denied Jesus three times and three different times Jesus asks Peter if he loved Him.

These questions made Peter not only an object of Grace but an instrument as well.

Jesus asks, *"Do you love me more than these?"*

Think about that question for a moment. Peter's mind had to be racing back to thoughts of "I'll follow you even to death, Jesus." But when death came for Jesus, Peter was denying any involvement with Him. That had to be a blow for Peter.

So Peter says, *"Yes, Lord; you know I love you."*

But there was no condemnation from Jesus, only Grace.

I can almost picture Jesus smiling to Peter and simply saying, *"Feed my lambs."*

In that one question Peter became both an object of Grace, and is realizing that he shall be an instrument of Grace for the rest of his life.

This is where I think many Christians lose foundational theology about Grace. We see it as an instant thing that hits us and saves us and then it goes on to the next person.

Grace is so much more than that.

As we've said earlier, Grace saves us, keeps us, empowers us, heals us, restores us, and delivers us. The very power of the resurrection becomes alive in us by Grace.

We have to realize Jesus freely extended Grace to Peter after the denial (an object of Grace), and then made Peter an extension of that same Grace and said, "feed my lambs" (an instrument of Grace.)

We all want to be objects of Grace. That's easy. I'll take a dose of that. My sins forgiven, a place in heaven (that's cool), but I'm not ready to actively engage the lives of others.

I'm not equipped for that.

If you believe that, you learned that from man and not the Word of God.

For some reason churchmen feel you have to earn your stripes before becoming the hands and feet of Christ.

The Bible however, does not teach that, and the examples of Grace in scripture almost counter that teaching.

If God can save you, then God will equip you to be an instrument of Grace to others.

Many leaders who are negative about this message of Grace only have a problem because of their fear of losing control.

Jesus dealt with those same issues with the religious leaders of His day, but those issues did not change Jesus' stance on the power of the Gospel of Grace and it should not change ours either.

Jesus said a second time, "Simon, son of John, do you love me?"

Jesus knew exactly how Peter felt towards Him. There was something deeper going on beneath the surface. Jesus was teaching a very important principle of Grace.

1.) A simple conversation with Jesus and **we become objects of His Glorious Grace.**

This happens in a moment, and we change.

So Peter said to him, "Yes, Lord; you know that I love you." And Jesus responds, "Tend my sheep."

2.) A simple conversation with Jesus and **we become instruments of His Glorious Grace.**

This is the beginning of a journey.

Jesus says you will be endowed with all you need for your task and there will always be sheep that need tending.

Jesus is building towards something HUGE.

He said to him the **third time**, *"Simon, son of John, do you love me?"*

I want to focus on this being the third time Jesus asked Peter this question.

Do you remember how many times Peter was asked if he knew Jesus, just before the crucifixion?

It was three times, with three wrong answers.

But Jesus did not ask three times to condemn.

This was to show that no matter what, if you love Christ, and you are willing to be honest with Him, Grace is always right there and you have instant access to the resurrection power of God.

Jesus knows how we feel about Him. He knows the questions we have, but asks us anyway.

He says, " _____ *do you love me?"*

No matter what has happened up to this point in your life, Jesus stands waiting for your answer.

If you are reading this book my hope is you have already answered yes.

The good news is that it does not end there.

If you love Christ and He is Lord of your life, you are an object of Grace. That happened in an instant.

Now He has something else to say to you.

"Feed my sheep."

You have been restored, now it is time you are re-instated.

Being an object of Grace takes a moment, but being an instrument of Grace takes a lifetime.

The apostle Paul says this…

1 Corinthians 15:8-11- *"Last of all, as to one untimely born, he (Jesus) appeared also to me. ⁹ For I am the least of the apostles, unworthy to be called an apostle, because I persecuted the church of God. ¹⁰* **But by the grace of God I am what I am, and his grace toward me was not in vain. On the contrary, I worked harder than any of them, though it was not I, but the grace of God that is with me** *¹¹ Whether then it was I or they, so we preach and so you believed."*

Paul was both an object and an instrument of God's Grace.

Peter was both an object and an instrument of God's Grace, and so are you.

And do you know what instruments do?

They make Rhythm.

About Rhythms of Grace

The book "Rhythms of Grace" started out as a post on Facebook©.

I had been praying for months about how to begin the task of writing a book on Grace. How would I do it justice? How would the message be received?

Then I saw a post from Meg (my wife) one morning and I knew I'd found it. Within this one portion of scripture is everything you need to know. Whether you are born again, or are far from God, this is for you.

Matthew 11:28-30

"Are you tired? Worn out? Burned out on religion? Come to me. Get away with me and you'll recover your life. I'll show you how to take a real rest. Walk with me and work with me—watch how I do it. Learn the unforced rhythms of grace. I won't lay anything heavy or ill-fitting on you. Keep company with me and you'll learn to live freely and lightly."

It's as simple as that. The work of the cross is a finished work. Rhythms of Grace is a real life picture of how that looks in our lives, each and every day. Grace takes our mind off how bad we are, and places our focus on how absolutely perfect Christ is. We don't need to be beat up by performance based religion. We need to embrace the cross that says, you can't re-do what's already been done.

"Jesus paid it all, all to Him I owe. Sin had left a crimpson stain, He washed it white as snow."

Elvina M. Hall 1865

When we realize what Grace cost Jesus, and what Grace offers us, then we will want nothing more than to live our lives to the "Praise of His Glorious Grace."

For more information about:

Small Group Curiculum

Speaking Engagements

Ordering copies of Rhythms of Grace

visit:

www.rhythmsofgrace.me

or email:
scott@rhythmsofgrace.me

@scottbryant2911

Made in the USA
San Bernardino, CA
17 April 2014